Borges

BORGES
An Introduction

JULIO PREMAT

Translated by AMANDA MURPHY

Vanderbilt University Press
Nashville, Tennessee

Copyright Presses Universitaires de Vincennes, Saint-Denis, 2018
English translation copyright 2021 Vanderbilt University Press
All rights reserved
First printing 2021

Library of Congress Cataloging-in-Publication Data

Names: Premat, Julio, author. | Murphy, Amanda, 1985–, translator.
Title: Borges : an introduction / Julio Premat ; translated by Amanda Murphy.
Description: Nashville : Vanderbilt University Press, [2021] | Originally published in French by Saint-Denis Presses universitaires de Vincennes in 2018. | Includes bibliographical references and index.
Identifiers: LCCN 2021016906 (print) | LCCN 2021016907 (ebook) | ISBN 9780826502261 (hardcover) | ISBN 9780826502254 (paperback) | ISBN 9780826502278 (epub) | ISBN 9780826502285 (pdf)
Subjects: LCSH: Borges, Jorge Luis, 1899–1986—Criticism and interpretation.
Classification: LCC PQ7797.B635 Z7988 2021 (print) | LCC PQ7797.B635 (ebook) | DDC 868—dc23
LC record available at https://lccn.loc.gov/2021016906
LC ebook record available at https://lccn.loc.gov/2021016907

CONTENTS

Introduction: A Classic of Modernity — 1

PART I. *A Single Sightless Self, a Plural I: Figures* — 7

1. The Works of a Hero — 11
2. The Son at Work — 33
3. The Clairvoyance of the Blindman — 60

PART II. *A Pensive Sentiment: Materials* — 85

4. Impelled by his Germanic Blood: Biography and the Meaning of the Story — 89
5. The Universe, *Whodunit?*: Reading and the Detective Novel — 103
6. The Library: Tradition, Betrayal, Transgression — 117
7. Forms of Eternity — 134

Notes   153
Bibliography   163

INTRODUCTION
A Classic of Modernity

IF JORGE LUIS Borges (1899–1986) has become one of the most emblematic writers of modern times, it is undoubtedly due to the acuity with which he raised issues surrounding originality, the past, and dialogue with cultural inheritance, as well as to the way he questioned the possibility of even being able to continue to write literature at a time when, according to Hannah Arendt, quotation and rewriting were becoming the only refuge, a time when tradition appeared to be broken and loss of the value of authority irreparable.[1] This crisis of culture and its transmission are accentuated in Borges by the peripheral location of his activity, in a country with a tenuous literary tradition at the beginning of the twentieth century; to become a writer, he had to create a tradition for himself and invent the means to legitimate his position before universal literature.

Like for Proust and Kafka, Borges turned "being an author" into a vital adventure, whether it be by way of the representation of an overtly mythical autobiography or the deployment of an existential perspective that engages with death, loss, alienation, and melancholy. For all three of these authors, writing is an arduous but invigorating task, while the question "What to write?" incessantly haunts. Their responses differ: Proust's profusion when faced with death, augmenting the textual mass with each correction of *Remembrance*...; the infinity and failure in the drastically unfinished state of Kafka's works; the allusion to imaginary books that one doesn't try to write but that bring us closer to the ideal of a Total Book in Borges. Their writing problematizes to exasperation the question of the subject (memory, duality, alienation) and that of the failed quest for the impossible, a form of *impossible* that might enter into dialogue with the fleeting past and with modern-day nightmares. Moreover, as with the Jewishness of Kafka, writing in German in Prague, the cultural and historical position of Borges—Argentina—did not facilitate the task for him, although the constraints of this location did impose decisions upon him that helped map out a literary singularity as paradoxical as it is extraordinary.

This is how Borges's work became the most important classic of Latin American literature in the canonic sense of the term (position within literary histories and curricula, a mandatory and highly respected reference in other forms of discourse); it is also due to the passion that characterizes the reception of Borges. Reading Borges is an experience that leaves an impression of a wealth of meaning and generates a kind of compulsive desire to interpret. The result, after sixty years of commentary on his work, is that critical production on him is beyond conceivable, or beyond decency, as we might say, paraphrasing the ironic tone of the writer.

If we take up Borges's own both iconoclastic and functional definition of the term, we can consider that he has been read as a "classic." For him, a classic is a book that for "various reasons generations of men read with anticipated fervor," imagining that "in its pages, everything [is] deliberate, fatal, profound, like the cosmos, and open to endless interpretations."[2] For his readers, Borges in and of himself is literature, all of literature: a life and a world of books, quotations and infinite paths through the library; an unrelenting attraction to the impact of words and worship of their aesthetic arrangement; a curiosity for everything surrounding imagination, metaphysics, dreams; and an apparent indifference to the politics of our human societies. Though this is not an entirely accurate state of affairs, as many texts contradict this idealized, autonomous, and elitist vision of an erudite Borges—large portions of his production establish an intense and complex dialogue with ideological constructions and forms of power[3]—these ideas are at the core of his image. To read Borges, enjoying Borges, is to enjoy thought, reflection, the imaginary, and literature, at least a certain conception of it, literature that conceives of man and of the world in close dialogue with the metaphysical.

In any event, the Borgesian work presents an extraordinary semantic plasticity and opens the way for a myriad of interpretations evoking historical references and ideas that could not be further from each other. He, who seemingly turned his back on his contemporaneity, who glorified the past and the scholarly tradition, who pled for a transhistoricity of literature, he who, in the middle of the twentieth century in Argentina, was spinning mythological tales and singing of Saxon warriors from the Middle Ages or reviving the marvels of *The Thousand and One Nights*, was also the emblem of all forms of modernity: transformational and parricidal avant-gardes, melancholic disarray before times of change, the questioning of the great traditional literary myths (the author, chronology, realism), generalized intertextuality, re-writings and pastiches, moderated skepticism, and the hypothesis of a universal literature.

In this hindered and complex process of becoming a writer that characterizes Borges, the great tradition of Western storytelling, namely, the novel from the end of the eighteenth century to the beginning of the twentieth, is in a way eluded. Despite his assiduous readings of Faulkner (whom he translated) and Kafka (him again), two great figures of genre renewal, Borges would find his filiation elsewhere. If he would become the great *narrator without a novel* of the twentieth century, it is because his models and rhetoric borrow from philosophy, theology, and forms unique to the encyclopedia, as well as from poetry, the Anglo-American short story, and even science fiction.

His writing is comprised of short, often-fragmentary texts that mix genres and constitute, in the end, an atypical corpus marked by multiple interventions during the publishing process and the republication of his books (at least until the establishment of *the* Book, the imposing volume of his complete works in Spanish published in 1974). This history of the publication of his works is indeed complex: first versions, revised editions, republications with inserted texts, prefaces and epilogues (sometimes quite decisive) with different dates, and so on. This is an area in which the strategy of the author is quite directly expressed: publishing, for him, meant building a writerly image and delimiting the contours of the work that he wanted to be read by eliminating the unnecessary and what interfered, and sometimes by adding interpretive and indexical possibilities. Under these conditions, it is quite difficult to determine the limits of the *complete* works of the author, which explains the numerous differences between the French version published by La Pléiade and the Argentine one put out by Emecé; these posthumous publications incorporate certain texts left aside by the author and yet neglect others published separately. While there exists a core set of important, widely recognized works, understanding of what is peripheral to it continues to be deficient; Borges's lifework today remains shifting and mobile.

The goal of this book is to provide an introduction to this authorial figure and to his works, in other words, to render highly complex phenomena comprehensible, while attempting to avoid simplifying their content, limiting their pertinence, or merely outlining their processes. This twofold constraint imposed certain decisions upon me. While not forsaking the big picture, I deemed it necessary to develop and put forth a hypothetical reading and, consequently, not to evoke every possible subject or all acceptable interpretations, and even less, all the connections between the works and their various intellectual and artistic contexts. While Gérard Genette summarized *Remembrance of Things Past* in one sentence, "Marcel becomes a writer,"[4] our itinerary here will be guided by a similar question: what stages and aesthetic choices lead to "becoming a writer," a process that, with Borges, is as problematic as it is structuring? The establishment of a kind of legendary autobiography will allow us to articulate the different stages of his lifework and to appreciate the many tensions that permeate it. After evoking the modalities of self-representation in the first part of the book, I will present in the second part several cross-cutting themes that, though not exhaustive, are in direct relation to the stages explored in the first part. English- and Spanish-speaking readers will find complementary bibliographies and a great deal of information on the website of the University of Pittsburgh's Borges Center, www.borges.pitt.edu.

A second decision that governs this book was made in light of the Borgesian bibliography available. There is, outside of the Hispanic world, a specific tradition of reading that tends to focus on certain aspects considered to be most coherent within French or Anglo-Saxon literary criticism and emphasizes the elements most relevant to it. In the average reading of Borges, certain periods of production and certain questions are sometimes neglected. I would like nonetheless to mention the existence of some major works available in English written by specialists of Argentine literature that offer sophisticated readings of Borges: *Signs of Borges* (1994) by Sylvia Molloy and *Borges: A Writer on the Edge* (1993) by Beatriz Sarlo; we must also remember the important critical production of Daniel Balderston, the current foremost specialist on the author (his most recent book as of this writing is *How Borges Wrote*, 2018). Following their example, I have tried here to accentuate the less known and less visible aspects, in particular Borges's relationship to the avant-garde, to traditional Argentine culture, and to the fame of his later years.

Furthermore, please take note of the aforementioned defining features of the Borgesian corpus and forgive me the many simplifications to the chronology of publications and the designation of dates of certain editions as definitive, even when sometimes these simplifications and choices are debatable. I thank Daniel Balderston and Federico Calle Jordá for their readings of the manuscript of this book.

PART I

A Single Sightless Self, a Plural I

Figures

Which of the two is setting down this poem—
a single sightless self, a plural I?

"Poem about Gifts," 1960[1]

Beginning a general presentation of Jorge Luis Borges with what resembles a biobibliographical history in chronological order may appear paradoxical. Indeed, one of the most spectacular particularities of the Argentine is the way he breaks apart linear time, questions the causal relationship of any temporal suite, and puts forth the ideas, every step of the way, that the past can be reinvented and transformed, and even that no time is ever entirely in the past. If we take this proliferation and this temporal instability literally, a chronological narrative would certainly be inappropriate.

Nonetheless, parallel to this forking and inversing of time, there is, in Borges, a self-figuration of a narrative kind that returns regularly to a limited number of anecdotes, events, and decisions (in 1925, he had already written, "All literature is, finally, autobiographical"[2]). Through the superposition of these biographemes or mythemes, if we want to use the academic terms, Borges offers up different images of himself that also serve as points of entry into his work. Paths that complete, become and extend the meaning, or non-meaning, of his books.

We will therefore read the three portraits that follow, and that refer quite loosely to three periods or three moments in Borges's life, as a gallery of possibilities rather than as a logical sequence. Even if these portraits correspond to the ages and inflections of Borges's journey, the writer, never forgetting or erasing them, took every opportunity to prolong them. The series of avatars of himself presented here does not indicate a series of changes, but rather an active accumulation that renders the Borgesian authorial figure increasingly complex: an authorial figure in the form of a story or of a multiplicity of mini-stories that functions as a place where the aporias and contradictions of his identity might be resolved, which is in fact a feature of every narrative identity.

CHAPTER 1

The Works of a Hero

A grandiose, vehement disbelief can be our great accomplishment.

"The Full Extent of My Hope," 1926[1]

Inventing Buenos Aires

"More than a city, Buenos Aires is a country, and we must find for it the poetry, the music, the painting, the religion, and the metaphysics appropriate to its grandeur. This is the full extent of my hope, which invites all of us to be gods and to work toward its incarnation."[2] The messianic intention of this call by Borges in 1926 (when he was twenty-seven) is quite surprising: finding a metaphysics and a religion for Buenos Aires, taking on the role of the gods, and proceeding, as they do, to incarnate. He had been participating for several years as a poet and essayist in the dynamic avant-garde movements and publications of 1920s Argentina.

This exhortation directed at the artists of his time to create together an aesthetic and spiritual Buenos Aires appears in "El tamaño de mi esperanza" ("The Full Extent of My Hope") the introductory text of his second book of essays (also titled *El tamaño de mi esperanza*, published in 1926; the first book of essays was *Inquisitions*, published in 1925); it comes after two volumes of poetry dedicated to the Argentine capital (*Fervor de Buenos Aires* in 1923 and *Luna de enfrente* [Moon across the way] in 1925). One of the major characteristics of the essays and poems assembled in these four works thereby becomes a sort of program, as we can read in them an exhilarating representation of certain aspects and certain specific areas of Buenos Aires. Borges, seeking his literary voice and personality at the time, chose to focus on the poetic particularities of what he called his "race," *criollez* (creoleness), in a mindset not without a certain literary nationalism.[3]

The call to invent an aesthetic and metaphysical Buenos Aires is directly related to the context of the 1920s, a decade of rapid mutations and radical aesthetics. The city Borges evokes had developed staggeringly thanks to forty years of massive immigration. The growth in its population went hand in hand with the modernization of its transportation system (the subway, for example, was inaugurated in 1913) and the rapid transformation of its urban make-up. Traditional Buenos Aires became, in a short time, a modern cosmopolitan metropolis, transformed by the sudden arrival of technology and a heterogeneous mass of foreigners; it then became the privileged backdrop and subject of young avant-garde artists' work, whether it be in poetry (Oliverio Girondo), the novel (Roberto Arlt), or painting (Xul Solar).

However, the Buenos Aires that Borges would "found" is not the one anchored in modernity, nor is it the one with a city center and colorful crowds of people, nor the one with big modern buildings and avenues swarming with cars and tramways, but the one with margins, outskirts, city limits, these flat and serene spaces where the city is in contact with the surrounding countryside and with the past (or according to him, sometimes, with a form of eternity); his space is the one he calls—as it is called in tango, the popular music of the time—the *arrabal* (the outskirts). In the very first poem ("The Streets") of his first book of poetry, *Fervor de Buenos Aires*, he writes:

> My soul is in the streets
> of Buenos Aires.
> Not the greedy streets

jostling with crowds and traffic
but the neighborhood streets where nothing is happening,
almost invisible by force of habit,
rendered eternal in the dim light of sunset.[4]

That is where Borges positions himself, in "streets where nothing is happening," in a form of marginality, at the edge, at a place that had been invisible up to then, and that he would propel, through a kind of elegy, toward the realm of the legendary, associating these spaces with the essence of the poet's identity ("my soul") and with creative subjectivity ("rendered eternal").

For him, the city to be founded, mixed in with his personal "Argentinity," the city destined to crystalize his identity as a writer was this city made up of unnamed streets, dark alleys, one-story houses that go on forever ("the drab houses, / the crude banisters, the doorknockers"[5]), local groceries, patios that open onto the immensity of the sky ("The patio is the slope / down which the sky flows into the house"[6]). It is in these everyday spaces that poetry emerges, poetry that comes about through the contemplation of "ancient stars" in an anonymous patio, surrounded by "the scent of jasmine and of honeysuckle / the silence of the sleeping bird, the arch of the entrance, the damp."[7] Poetry is marked by epiphany when, after long strolls through the peripheral neighborhoods, twilight turns everything into aesthetic signs and symbols ("and I saw in the depths / the colored sunset like a game of cards / and I felt Buenos Aires"[8]). These few quotes from *Fervor de Buenos Aires*, the book whose title, as we have seen, is highly programmatic, could be multiplied in reading his other poetry volumes published around the same time.

The incantations cited tend in any case to be reactions, in advance, to the observation made in "The Full Extent of My Hope": "Our vital reality is grandiose and our thought reality is impoverished";[9] they seek, through repetition, the use of a vocabulary of the sacred, and aestheticizing mechanisms, to delimit a place inhabited by individuals called upon to become *topoï* in his subsequent writings (*topoï* included in his legendary "The South"—both of the city and of the country—to which he assiduously referred until the end of his life). From this landscape emerges a type of character (the *malevo*, the crook, the thug) and a legendary action, the duel with knives, both of which are called upon to become the most recurrent subjects of his writing—in 1955 he would affirm that "Our myth is the duel with knives."[10]

Borges shares these spaces and this mythology of the intimate with popular poetry and with the lyrics of tangos, which are also anchored in the suburbs.[11] In his texts, he positions himself, however, as a pioneer, a founder; he was, supposedly, the first to see the city in this way, he, who in the alleyways faced with the immensity of the sky, would come to experience a transcendental revelation.[12] On one hand, he observes the poverty of Argentine literature ("These lands have not engendered a mystic [. . .] not one feeler or understander of life!"[13]) and on the other, he dramatizes the arrival of his own texts. Texts that are supposed to say something new, which has never been said, the beauty of the "urban landscape not yet soiled by verbiage."[14] At the end of his life and of his lifework, in the preface he wrote for the Bibliothèque de la Pléiade edition dated May 19, 1986 (Borges died on June fourteenth), he yet again evoked the utopia of unique, inaugural language: "Each new page is an adventure in which we must take risks. Each word is the first word spoken by Adam."[15]

The role attributed to the *pampa* and to its hypostasis, the *gaucho*, reinforces this orientation: "The pampa and *Suburbio* are gods," he wrote in another essay from the same period.[16] If this enthusiastic elegy of the outskirts of the city would come to nourish a kind of nationalism, it is through its association with a precise space-time, the pampa of the nineteenth century, the place of civil wars and the *gauchesca* (a poetry form inspired by popular culture and country living) that Borges read from childhood on. A pampa that, too, was overtly fabled, elevated to the function of defining referent by the nationalism of the beginning of the twentieth century, thanks, in particular, to a few foundational texts such José Hernández's narrative poem *Martín Fierro* (1872–1879), which marks the height of the *gauchesca*. Borges then adhered to what he called "creolism": the promotion of characters and customs, assumed to be authentic, associated in Argentina with this pampa of the nineteenth century and with the use of specific vocabulary and variants of Spanish. His point of view from the outskirts of the city allowed for the heroic past of the pampa to penetrate the new Buenos Aires, tradition migrating from the countryside to the suburbs and bringing depth to the modern and indistinguishable city, therein endowing it with a legend.

These peripheral places were called, in Borgesian criticism (by Beatriz Sarlo and Jean-Philippe Barnabé for example) and by Borges himself, the *orillas* (banks, fringes, borders). Just as the pampa of the nineteenth century, an empty space—the pampa refers to a herbaceous plain without any landforms or distinctive traits—would become a defining symbol, Borges would transform the bleak suburbs into an artistic and metaphysical "incarnation"; he would invent, in a way, these margins of the city in order to turn them into a territory invested with meaning, as much for him as for the collective within which he was writing. In 1921, he had already anticipated this gesture: "What is beautiful is what is marginal. For example any house in the *arrabal*";[17] in one of these houses, any one of them, he announced, "our Saviour" will be born,[18] in other words, the literary prophet that Argentina needed.

Founding a Work

This series of decisions and series of texts constitutes the most well-known and the most spectacular aspect of Borges's beginnings; it is an entry into literature that pointedly identifies the problems surrounding his connection to national belonging, as well as those surrounding the possibility of differentiated creation in the *orillas*—those other suburbs, those in the West, where Argentina is located. The whole of the opinions on the matter form a nodal point in the most famous text from this poetic corpus of Borges's youth, "The Mythical Founding of Buenos Aires."[19] In this poem from the collection *Cuaderno San Martín* [San Martin notebook], Borges rewrites, in a narrative and ironic tone, the foundation of the city of Buenos Aires in 1536—in reality, an ephemeral fort abandoned in 1541. A second founding comes shortly after this first page in the city's history, that of the literary suburbs explored in his poetry and therefore of the emergence of an artificial Buenos Aires, nonetheless effective in terms of the imaginary produced. After witnessing the arrival of the Spanish, the reader sees the different elements of the suburbs that Borges has already typified in his previous poems "flourish" without any sort of continuity (the pink-walled grocer, the cardplayers, the street corner, the local bully, the Barbarian organ player, tangos, the first political orders).

The operation is vertiginous: we go from a neutral and incredulous version of how the actual city was founded to the self-made foundation of a literary space, a space that the author intends to mythicize himself (it is indeed, as the title indicated, a "mythical foundation.") The final outcome of the poem highlights this explicit operation and gives it a general meaning: "The afternoon had established its yesterdays / and men took on together an illusory past."[20] Thus, thanks to this second foundation, the new city possesses historical depth ("yesterdays"), and men and women now share a past invented before their eyes. Borges thus responds to the need expressed in "The Full Extent of My Hope": a literary, mythical, symbolic Buenos Aires is created. The last two lines of "The Mythical Founding" ultimately erase all trace of factual historicity as well as of literary invention: "Hard to believe Buenos Aires has any beginning. / I feel it to be as eternal as air and water."[21] The city is located both in fiction (its beginning is made up of "stories" in the sense of fables or tales) and in an eternity perceived spontaneously as that of the elements, like that which we attribute to beauty and art.

We can perceive here an isomorphism between the gesture of founding a city and that of an entry into literature: the first stone is the first poem. On Valéry and Whitman, Borges would say, much later, that their works are "less valuable as poetry than as the mark of an exemplary poet who was himself created by it";[22] it is obvious here that he was taking on a similar task: creating a poet by inventing a city ("Borges creates the *suburbio*—the *arrabal* of Buenos Aires—in order to transform it into an anecdotal metaphor for the Self put to the task of affirming and denying itself"[23]).

To become a writer, to occupy a space, one must delimit a distinct place of belonging, even more so since Borges was brought up in his father's English library and at a Genevan high school. He counted on a "tender and irrevocable immortality" (he would write in 1927), which is that of "poets whose name is associated with a place in the world."[24] In this sense, we can inscribe Borges within an American tradition of inventing a space as a prerequisite to defining a narrative identity (William Faulkner, Juan Carlos Onetti, Gabriel García Márquez, and Juan José Saer are well-known examples of this). His position consisted in turning the ordinary—those bleak neighborhoods—into the extraordinary, in making the borderlands his own as if they were potentially the future center of literature, and in associating the writer's body and subjectivity with these streets and these houses. In doing so, the singularity of the young Borges took shape, a singularity that at first sight appears to be contradictory to the claims found in his later works. As we know, Borges would eventually leave *criollez* and the quest for the "national" behind, but the messianism that allowed him to invent universes and cosmic apparatuses (such as the imaginary world that replaces our own in "Tlön, Uqbar, Orbis Tertius" or the apotheosis of a temporal and spatial totality in "'The Aleph," short stories from the 1940s) would never leave him. Paradoxically, in this writer who rewrites with unparalleled originality, heroic foundation is a constant.

The self-portrait is quite present in this evocation of a marginal Buenos Aires: for example the story of returning to his country in 1921 would be revisited in many texts from this period and in subsequent texts ("After years of exile / I returned to the house of my childhood"[25]). Indeed, the Borges family moved to Geneva in 1914 where they would stay throughout the war; Jorge Luis, or rather Georgie as he was called in the family circle, studied at the Calvinist school of Geneva before spending a long period of time in Spain (first in Majorca, then in Seville and Madrid), which would allow Borges to frequent the Spanish avant-garde movements. As a counterpoint to the movement of return comes a discovery, a revelation, a novelty that, in a way, came from the past: "This city that I believed to be my past / is my future, my present; / the years that I spent in Europe are illusory, / I was always (and always will be) in Buenos Aires."[26]

On this homecoming, after mentioning the *Queen Victoria* that brought him back to Argentina and the date of his arrival, in his autobiography, he reminisces on his first impressions as if he were seeing the city with a panoramic view from the ship: "It came to me as a surprise, after living in so many European cities [...] to find that my native town had grown, and that it was now a very sprawling and almost endless city of low buildings with flat roofs, stretching west toward what geographers and literary hands call the pampa. It was more than a homecoming; it was a rediscovery. I was able to see Buenos Aires keenly and eagerly because I had been away from it for a long time. Had I never gone abroad, I wonder whether I would ever have seen it with the peculiar shock and glow that it now gave me."[27] This feeling of shock and glow, which is not too different from the epiphanies the suburbs would later produce in him, is a precursory sign of the beginning of a work, a beginning coded in biographical experience and endowed with an epic dimension.

Writing in Other Ways

Nonetheless, the delimitation of a literary Buenos Aires and the heroic prowess of its foundation are far from exhausted in Borges's productions of the 1920s because, among other things, the young writer who arrived in March 1921 (he had just turned twenty-two) did not come empty-handed. In his intellectual baggage, in addition to the reading he had done in English, French, and German during his stay in Europe, he brought with him the avant-gardes. Or at least, such is the common, but quite exaggerated, version of the story, since Borges was neither the only traveler nor the only line of communication. It was desirable to attribute to Borges the role of introducing these movements, in part due to the insistence with which he evoked first his European youth and the literary dynamism of his return. In Argentine literary history, he therefore plays the role of the prophet of the "new sensitivity."

Be that as it may, while in Spain, Borges did become friends with two figures of reference for young Iberians: the older writers Rafael Cansinos Assens and Ramón Gómez de la Serna. The radicality of this period makes it difficult to find continuity with his later evolution, in particular due to the political ideas that would lead him to begin a collection of poems dedicated to the glory of the Russian Revolution (*Red Rhythms*) and to defend the Dada movement in Spain (with some friends, he even experimented with provocative and vaguely obscene automatic writing). This was also a period of passionate reading and of pioneering translations of German expressionist poets. And finally, above all, it was a period of collective experiences and publications on and within the Ultraist movement, which he would attempt to promote in the Argentine capital.

Ultraism, created among the entourage of Cansinos Assens, revisited the critiques, typical of the time, of inherited literature and affirmed a desire for renewal, with the ardor of an "eternal youth" that can be found in absolute synchrony, in the "promise of advancing at the same speed as time." Borges, in an article from December 1921, "Ultraísmo," quotes Cansinos Assens and then presents his personal version of the movement. Ultraism rejected post-symbolist or modernist (in the Hispanic sense of the term) "verbosity"; in other words, it sought to eliminate empty sentences and useless embellishments and demanded, above all, an innovative use of metaphor: poetry had to be made of complex, previously unseen, superimposed images. Originality therefore consisted in creating metaphors that revealed unexpected analogies;[28] finding it was a pressing task (in a 1924 text he explains that faced with the "urgent beauty of the world relentlessly asking us to place it in our lines of poetry," he "met" metaphor "and it was the exorcism thanks to which we could sow confusion in the rigid universe"[29]).

Although Borges quickly distanced himself from the Ultraist *doxa*, his first few years in Buenos Aires were characterized by feverish literary activity in continuity with his European experiences. He would found no fewer than three literary magazines, one of which took on the form of a mural, and would collaborate with all the other major avant-gardist publications of the time. However, in terms of organic belonging or aesthetic adhesion to any one movement or group, there is not much, we must admit: three or four years in the life of a young man. As early as 1925, in *Inquisitions*, ironic critiques of the avant-garde can already be found.

Interested as he was in the conditions required for literary triumph, his attraction to aesthetic audacity would nonetheless remain, along with a certain lucidity with regard to the conditions of success. For radicalism and excess are not incompatible with the idea of a "career"; for example, in an essay on the Spanish baroque poet Góngora (sixteenth and seventeenth centuries), considered to be sophisticated and hermetic, Borges affirmed that Góngora committed certain aesthetic errors with full awareness that the exhibition of new discursive means better ensured notoriety than would reasonable stylistic invention. The writer knew that "failures, as long as they pretend to have a method to their folly, can become renowned. Example: Góngora. Example: every writer of our time on any page."[30] Experimentation, even if it is merely a means to an end and does not necessarily indicate aesthetic progress, can guarantee a spot in literary history. And Borges knew it.

The messianic dimension of his project, which manifests itself primarily in the foundation of Buenos Aires as we have just observed, is also part of the libertarian spirit of the time. Beyond the experience with Ultraism—visible in his personal use of metaphor—certain questions raised by the movement resurface frequently in essays written later. Borges was clearly attracted to a certain formalism linked to this quest for new rhetoric and therefore to the avant-gardes.

However, none of this is foreign to the stylistic practices of the poets and narrators of the Spanish Golden Age (Góngora, and especially Quevedo, a writer whom Borges admired immensely). The result in his texts is, in part, a complex repertoire of analogies that seek to surprise the writer "Standing like an archangel, the setting sun / tyrannized the path"[31]; "From curved shoulders / came rifles and viaducts."[32] Furthermore, his prose would not only be "creolizing," but also, in his manner, "baroquizing," full, as it is, of rhetorical operations, neologisms, and unusual or forced syntactical constructions whose model was, above all, none other than the prose of Quevedo.

The strong but ambivalent attraction to Ultraism can be linked to another consistent desideratum, the will to invent a language, be it national or literary, from which stems the persistent fascination for glossolalia that we find in many of his later short stories and essays. Moreover, the structured reflections and occasional allusions to the value of metaphor are frequent in all his books, both as a way to make clear his stance on his Ultraist youth and as a means to question the literality or the historicity of poetic discourse. At the time, the question of a "national language" and more broadly, of lexical and syntactical innovation tirelessly occupied him in what appears to be a prolonged intention to establish a place of belonging. Face to face with *his* Buenos Aires, it was a matter of finding *his* style, a style that would correspond to his reality and that would be as unprecedented as his city.

Yet, like everything in Borges, his personal objectives and the aesthetic premises of his writing would take on a universal scope. In addition to his call to found Buenos Aires, the texts included in *El tamaño de mi esperanza* constitute a coherent series with regard to linguistic innovation, the invention of words, the use of adjectives, and the qualities and limits of *lunfardo* (Argentine slang), which underscores their importance. The same goes for the other two collections of essays from the 1920s (*Inquisitions* and *The Language of the Argentines*). As a general rule, it is a matter of getting distance from the Spanish of Spain, loosely associated with a literature of the past (it too, bygone), which is the reason for the title of one of his books, *The Language of the Argentines*.

However, the issue lay not only in positing the particularism of a national language, but rather in highlighting its freshness and the newness of the language itself. Writers must, he affirmed, be aware that the language is in a state of a kind of first draft; consequently, they have the "glorious" choice; they have the duty to breed it and to propose variations of it.[33] In this sense, metaphoric creation crystalizes in an innovative program: the metaphor emerges palliative to the poverty of the inherited language and symbolizes, on a microtextual level, the will to write differently. The case of nouns, for example, is, for him, significant; they weaken expression as they introduce a kind of dissimulation: "instead of saying cold, sharp, biting, unbreakable, shining, pointed, we say dagger."[34] If any and every word, although succinct, encompasses in itself a myriad of characteristics, this simplifying convention allows for the writer to imagine other enunciative solutions.

Naturally, these premises led the way to a baroque style although Borges's subsequent prose, on the contrary, privileges sober, precise expression not without resonance with what the French tradition calls *le mot juste*. Nonetheless, the question of the metaphor, which has its roots in Borges's adherence in youth to Ultraism, can be found throughout his work; taking on various meanings and forms, it nonetheless reveals a constant inquiry into originality and the power of personal creation, as well as a complex negotiation process with inherited forms. The most famous statement on this point figures in "Pascal's Sphere," an essay included in *Other Inquisitions*, in which he proposes a transhistoricity of analogies: "Perhaps universal history is only the history of a few metaphors."[35] In "Nathaniel Hawthorne" of the same collection, he insists: "The real ones [metaphors], those that formulate intimate connections between one image and another, have always existed; those we can still invent are the false ones, which are not worth inventing."[36]

More generally, and to complete the portrait painted by Borges's youthful avant-gardist posture of the time, we could not fail to mention the inclination toward the systematic revision of literary myths and beliefs, and consequently, toward a certain irreverence or even insolence. Despite the ceremonial phrases at work in his essays, Borges's literary and metaphysical ideas are based on an impertinent destabilization of certainties. Accordingly, even if the prescriptive nature of the literary opinions of his youth would disappear, the judgmental tone apparent in his first three books of essays (with each step he draws borders, arranges, rejects, delimits, proposes) would later become a remarkable penchant for unusual hierarchies, unexpected verdicts, and mocking anathema. Along the same lines, perhaps the role of humor and the attraction to ironic dissimulation throughout his work are not incongruent to his beginning as a writer or to his provocations, playful or not, of the avant-gardist movements; in any case, during these years, he was already practicing a renewed form of an old baroque technique, positioning oneself at the cutting edge.

But if anything should be retained from Borges's avant-garde period, it would perhaps be his strong liking for argumentative confrontation, literary battles, and murderous irony. Antagonism reveals itself in Borges as a sort of migration of the duel with knives—his favorite fictional adventure—into literary battle. The attraction to conflict, inherent in the figure of the hero, would accompany him throughout his life, even if other images, like that of the modest librarian or the wisest of blindmen, sometimes overshadow it. The young Borges manifests an epic of confrontation—that is generational—thanks to what Alan Pauls appropriately calls "books as weapons."[37] Aggression is omnipresent and the polemical diatribes are extremely efficient.

The great canonical poet of the time, Leopoldo Lugones, bore the brunt of it when Borges wrote in *El tamaño de mi esperanza* a review of Lugones's latest poetry book, *Romancero*: "In this book, don Leopoldo Lugones proves himself to be almost no one, very clumsy, very free with the stuffing."[38] A few years later, his fourth collection of essays would bring opposition to the forefront with the title (*Discussion*, 1932); he would even write an "Art of Insult" (included in *A History of Eternity* in 1936). Later, in his stories, the controversies would continue, whether it be a duel with knives or an intellectual debate that turned into a life-threatening confrontation (as in "The Theologians" in *The Aleph* [1949] in which the rivalry between two theologians brings them to their deaths). It is an obsession: in these last collections of stories, the subject is omnipresent; for example, in *Brodie's Report* (1970), eight of the eleven stories that make up the collection are varying degrees of reformulations of artistic controversies and fights to the death. The voluminous journal of his friend Bioy Casares, who rigorously reproduced Borges's daily positions and commentaries over a significant period (1947–1986), reveals the consistency and acuity of the phenomenon. Heroic opposition and self-affirmation are pervasive whether it be in explicit or less obvious ways; in Borges, the definition of personal place, style, and tone is accomplished through combat. This combat is ultimately that of literary glory, which he often ponders—and delivers—in the essays of his youth.

It is safe to say that if Borges briefly ventured into the avant-garde, what he extracted from this experience was his foundational heroism, without integrating its maximalism or its dogmatism; he would proceed rather with the forcefulness of his youth, the impetus, the ardor that aimed to displace canonical literary references. Nonetheless, after having frequented a certain version of Borges as a pioneer, an inaugurator, we could list the examples that point to young Borges as already encyclopedic, he who uses Milton and Quevedo to discuss the originality of the poetry of his time,[39] or he who admits that his recent readings hardly excite him;[40] in his first book of essays, he was already mocking those who considered him to be "worm-eaten by old things."[41] We will come back to these inconsistencies surrounding erudition; but for the moment let's consider—as it will be the case for all future affirmations—that each step and each statement of Borges's questions itself, integrates its contrary, and even its antinomy; years later, in the description of the literature of the invented land of Tlön, he would write: "A book that does not contain its counter-book is considered incomplete."[42] Of course, this is a mere exaggerated image of his own position and of his own writing.

Finding Filiation

Throughout the whole of his trajectory, Borges was accompanied by some important people who, like brokers, escorted his ideas and aesthetic transformations. The hero that wanted to found a language, a place, and a position for himself compensates for—and prolongs—his radicalism by inscribing it in a complex system of filiation. Or, to put it another way, there is no hero without heroic identification. It is therefore appropriate to conclude by evoking two figures that played a fundamental role in the early years of Borges's entry into literature: Macedonio Fernández and Evaristo Carriego. In consonance with other elements already highlighted, these two figures are both, in different ways, outsiders: placing them in the role of master or model entails, here too, considering the *orillas* in progressive movement toward centrality.

Borges often repeated that at the time of his return in 1921, alongside the splendid discovery of Buenos Aires and with it, the arrival of a promising avant-garde, came something else. Before moving on to the major changes to his lifework that would take place during the 1930s, let us evoke this "something else," a final complementary image. The third image is that of Macedonio Fernández, a writer friend of Borges's father who met him at the dock upon his return; at the port, before Borges, lay a city transformed, but there was also the encounter with this intellectual, standing facing the river and the European experience that the young man was bringing back to Argentina. This is another foundational anecdote: "Perhaps the major event of my return was Macedonio Fernández."[43] From then on, Macedonio (he is known by his first name in Argentine literary history) would be given a prominent position in the complex network of referential figures and heroic identifications that Borges would construct over the years, sometimes changing the names, but never the functions.

Macedonio is an atypical, eccentric, marginal writer besotted with speculation, a sporadic reader and a comedian à la Bernard Shaw; in this respect, he wrote strange books that, although quite literary, orbit around philosophy and even psychology. Though he wrote a lot and often referred to his own projects, he rarely published, which would lead Borges to say that Macedonio was above all an oral writer, a *"porteño"* Socrates ("His genius survives in but a few of his pages; his influence was of a Socratic nature"[44]). The vehemence with which Borges would lay claim to this figure and to his influence, and exalt his intelligence and imagination would lead to Macedonio being seen, for quite some time, as a "creation" of Borges, a kind of appropriation: Borges was then, to continue the analogy, Macedonio's Plato (it should be noted in passing that the analogy tends paradoxically to diminish the role of the elder who becomes dependent on the writing and triumph of the novice: Socrates would not exist without Plato).

In any case, Borges's fascination with Macedonio promptly became evident; he would affirm for example that Macedonio was the most remarkable man he had met in his life.[45] He would attribute to him a way of reading, with skepticism, that would transform the impetuous but naïve youth into an established writer, lucid and skeptical. Macedonio's idealism, inspired by Berkeley and Schopenhauer, as well as his theories on the cancelation of the self and on the emptying of the subject, would leave a mark on much of the young Borges's writing, an example being the 1922 essay "The Nothingness of Personality," in which he formulates for the first time a frontal attack on the unity of the self, an idea which is given much development in his works.[46] One of the pillars of Borges's writing, the discovery of the narrative potentialities of philosophy, can be most surely traced to Macedonio, or in any case, his influence is one of the anecdotes that Borges makes use of to explain it; on other occasions, he recalls that his father showed him the Eleatic paradox of Achilles and the Turtle with the help of checker pieces.

Macedonio, with his ironic sense of humor, would become, in the 1920s and in large part thanks to Borges, a referential figure for young Argentine avant-gardists, a bit like Apollinaire in France, although he was in fact much more radical than any of them: his novel *The Museum of Eterna's Novel*, published in the 1960s, is not only the most important Latin American avant-gardist novel, but it's also a perfect example of what we could call "extreme writing." Thanks to this, and to his unique relationship to philosophy, Macedonio has come, in the last thirty years, to gain recognition in Argentine literature beyond his association with Borges and, in a way, despite it: the work of the master has finally diminished the mark left by the disciple.

The second figure is different: Evaristo Carriego is an unknown and minor poet; he too was a friend of the Borges family, and died prematurely in 1912. His work, brief and kept at a distance from aesthetic polemics, can be characterized by repeated references to the humble neighborhoods of Buenos Aires and to the private lives of their inhabitants. He would be completely forgotten today if Borges had not published a sort of biography of him (*Evaristo Carriego* in 1930). He saw in him, as he would explain much later, the discoverer of "the literary possibilities of the run-down and ragged outskirts of the city—the Palermo of [his] boyhood."[47]

At this time, Borges wanted to write "an important book on an entirely Argentine subject" and, thanks to Carriego, paint a longer-standing picture of the "Buenos Aires of yesteryear";[48] from the start, the goal was to go beyond the biographical, which is reduced here to the function of a catalyst, if not an alibi. The poet from the suburbs is raised up among the ranks of the founder and given an equivalent place to that which Borges would claim for himself, in a kind of reverse lineage. Obviously, all this indirectly painted a self-portrait and set the premises for an operation that would become much more regular: interested, instrumental, and strategic reading. Carriego, after all, matters little; he is but a displaced symbol of certain aspects of the literary personality that Borges was building for himself at the time: an outsider, a minor poet, even an unknown poet, capable nonetheless of transmitting the essence of an identity.[49] But the operation did not go on without a hitch: the challenge consisted in reinforcing the symbolic weight of the suburbs through the choice of an unknown and unimportant writer—who would become a precursor. What's more, the new mythology of Buenos Aires integrates in this book the neighborhood where Borges grew up, Palermo, which is symbolically central to the imaginary topography of the Borgesian city, of which Carriego would become the prime voice.

The result is a heterogeneous work in which the evocation of a legendary Palermo is connected to the life story of the poet and to the analysis of a few of his texts. *Evaristo Carriego* is complemented with several chapters on what could be called "popular poetry," in other words the lyrics to tangos, the mottos written in the barrows going back and forth across the city, the oral spirit and creativity that manifested itself during the most popular game of cards in Argentina, *truco*. Once again, we find the couplet city/discourse or place/language reinforced this time through the authority of a tutelary figure. The attraction to popular culture, paraliterature, and orality is accepted and would remain part of Borges's work.

Both Carriego and Macedonio are part of a chosen literary lineage that serves a specific function: adopting the poet from the suburbs who occupies no place in literary history (Carriego); adopting the extravagance of an iconoclastic figure (Macedonio). Both actions carve out a space for Borges detached from tradition, but both are also—here and elsewhere, ambivalence is foundational—as we have said, friends of the author's father. The question of centers and peripheries, rupture and continuity, and foundation and displacement perpetuate a filial situation and a family background; this is how the "(auto)biographeme of fathers"[50] operates. In his self-foundation, Borges is respectful of his elders.

The opposition Carriego/Macedonio, as well as the ambivalence that turned the young writer into both a sophisticated erudite and a pugnacious polemist drawn to mannish confrontation, truculent action, and rough neighborhoods, bring us to another mytheme, already present at this stage, but one that would develop and come to play a central role over the years to come, double lineage, for the autobiographical fabulations are motivated by Borges's origins, which are not only the object of a dense family history but which also, in accordance with the *topos* just evoked, display contradiction, opposition, and tension.

His paternal grandfather, Colonel Francisco Borges, was a soldier killed in combat during the civil wars of the nineteenth century; his mother came from a longstanding creole family whose ancestors also included military who participated in certain of the armed conflicts that have marked Argentine history. Taken sometimes by a certain enthusiasm, Borges enjoyed expanding on this line of descent by saying that he descended from conquistadors and that among his ancestors was a man who arrived in America with Juan de Garay during the definitive foundation of Buenos Aires in 1580. This is the epic side of his family history, constantly brought up to date through a great number of somewhat elegiac poems.

On the other side of his family, his paternal grandmother, Fanny Haslam, was a rather well-read English woman. Thanks to her, English would become the second language of Borges's home. Jorge Borges, his father, was an intellectual, a professor of psychology, a connoisseur of poetry and philosophy, an anarchist, a friend of writers. The library in which Borges says he was raised was his father's, a library with countless books in English; the father's fate as a failed writer was determinant in the life of his son, for it was always understood that Georgie would take the place of Don Jorge as a writer. This is, obviously, the mythical justification for Borges's most well-known predilections, his attraction to speculation and to philosophy, his love of books, and his subsequent passion for libraries.

Author Ricardo Piglia extracts from this double genealogy a broken, dispersed story that can be read as the story of Borges's writing.[51] This narrative on ancestors can be connected, on one hand, to the lineage of founders and warriors associated with the pampa of the nineteenth century and with an epic history, and on the other hand, to the lineage of his well-read intellectual ancestors, as well as that of writers and philosophers, all of whom Borges chose as adoptive fathers and who would become his precursors, his models. Familial relationships are, in Borges, metaphors for all the other relationships and constitute the pillars of a myth that does not in any way resolve its contradictions but retains them and makes a story out of them. This story therefore highlights a double belonging: the heritage of a military past and of foundational gestures, and that of the library and universal culture. These are, Piglia concludes, the properties that made Borges's writing possible.

Youthful Mistakes

In the corpus commented upon, there is an obvious connection between the writer's agenda and the messianic intention of the avant-garde (artists must be gods, as it was desired by one of the great figures of Latin American poetry identifying with Ultraism, Vicente Huidobro). A connection can also be made to a certain boldness in the act of consciously building a future, founding a different kind of artistic and metaphysical space. The prophetic word that brought novelty thanks to a paradoxical recovery of the past, the central role attributed to the author in the process, and the repeated recourse to the realm of the legendary provide the first sketches of Borges's self-portrait. In this period, we observe an assertive heroism and a series of attitudes that derive from it (insolence, confrontation, humor, disbelief, strategic marginality, and choosing one's own filiations).

Nonetheless, each element in this enumeration must be nuanced, or even contradicted. What characterizes Borges's messianic desire compared to so many other futurist projects of the time, the other great trait or discovery of this first period, is the inclusion of contraries and apparent tensions. On one hand, renovation, radical change, and invention; on the other, worship of the past, recovery of tradition, and the appropriation of somewhat outdated symbolic systems (creoleness and the pampa). For Borges, combat, insolence, the invention of language, novelty, and foundation go along with nostalgia, fascination with tradition, negativity, and pessimism. And he is aware of this. At the end of "The Full Extent of My Hope," he affirms seeking a quirky form of creoleness: "*Criollismo* by all means, but a *criollismo* that converses with the world and with the individual and with God and with death";[52] the act of exposing contradiction allows him to later superimpose a form of localism and an aggressive cosmopolitanism. And this is not the only tension visible in the process, since the pioneer messianism and the enthusiastic will to found are accompanied by disbelief, which in no way intimidates him. He states that "a grandiose, vehement disbelief can be our great accomplishment."[53] This double goal, rather than destroying the system or weakening it, turns it into a changing dynamic ensemble, more difficult to interpret but efficient.

This period is well known for many reasons: of course, thanks to the wealth of criticism on Borges and to the interest that Argentine commentators took in this period during which key questions included the debate over national or cosmopolitan literature, the conflict between popular and erudite cultures, and the possibility of innovative literature produced in the periphery of the Western world. But above all, Borges's youth is well known for the insistence with which the author discussed it throughout his life, in his fiction, as well as in his poems, essays, and numerous public appearances made at the end of his life. Each step of the way, he returns to his search for originality and innovation on one hand, and to his *criollez* on the other.

Yet early on, these references are made with an obvious counterpoint; the allusions to these beliefs and excesses are always accompanied by criticism, negation, or irony. Among the numerous examples, let us turn to the most spectacular one, furthest from Borges's biography. In "Averroes's Search" (*The Aleph*, 1949), twelfth century Muslim intellectuals in Spain debate like Argentine avant-gardists over metaphors; some believe in the need to "renew old metaphors" while the wise man Averroes defends the validity of great inherited analogies (such as that which compares the fate of man to a blind camel), which are not to be invented but rediscovered.[54] Here like elsewhere, the figure of the young Borges, naïve and impetuous, at the antipodes of the mature Borges, is indirectly mistreated. If the mythification of the writer appears in the texts of the 1920s, quite rapidly this self-exaltation would cede to its contrary, self-criticism, with the *topos* of "youthful mistakes."[55]

Nonetheless, all such simplified statements must once again be nuanced. On the one hand, indeed, Borges forbade that the three collections of essays commented on in this chapter (*Inquisitions*, *El tamaño de mi esperanza*, and *The Language of the Argentines*) be included in the first edition of his *Complete Works* (published in Spanish in 1974) and justified to great extent his refusal to re-edit them. They would only be known to the public after his death in 1986, during the dynamic of compulsive publication that took place at the time. Along the same lines, in the two main republications established during his lifetime (1943 and 1969), he made an enormous number of corrections to the three books of poetry of the 1920s (*Fervor de Buenos Aires*, *Luna de enfrente*, and *Cuaderno San Martín*), deleting some poems, rewriting others, and even, occasionally adding some. Through retrospective changes to his literary beginnings, he performs a transformation of the past: he rewrites his own story. For example, many of the quotations chosen for this chapter are the result of late changes; to simplify the presentation and the readability, I have not specified the historicity of the texts. I made this decision also because, in the end, it is the later vision, the modification of his youth to better endow it with meaning, that matters.

The changes made to his poems and collections are commented on, in the form of a programmatic affirmation, in the prologues written in 1969. These texts aimed to influence reception; they also defined the type of writer that Borges wanted to be, through the critique of the writer that he had been and no longer was. As elsewhere, and as is often the case, skeptical vision or lucid irony allowed for hidden praise, or for the indication of a preference or a desired readerly orientation. In these prologues he criticizes the excesses of his youth and makes a little fun of himself, in particular of his self-imposed desire to be modern ("To be modern is to be contemporary of our own time; inevitably, we must be so"[56]), or considers his nationalist ambition a paradox: "Forgetting that I already was, I wanted to be Argentinian."[57] Sometimes he goes even further, establishing radical distance, affirming nonrecognition between the old Borges and the young one, presented as the author of texts that "feel foreign" to him; consequently he is not "affected by their errors nor by their potential virtues."[58] He even asserts that he only "slightly modified these two works" (*Luna de enfrente* and *Cuaderno San Martín*) which is a false statement: between 1943 and 1969, he removed ten poems from these short collections and added two. The reason is simple: "They are no longer mine," he explained.[59]

The distance taken mythologizes, conversely, the young man enthralled in his epic plans and serves in turn to put forth a certain conception of the role of an author and of the nonvalidity of his plans or of his will. However, in the same 1969 edition, this time discussing *Fervor de Buenos Aires*, he writes, "the young man who wrote the book in 1923" is essentially "the mature author who either resigns himself never to touch his earlier work or who endeavors to rewrite it. We both are the same person; neither of us believes in either failure or success or in literary cabals and their dogmas; both are fond of Schopenhauer, Stevenson, and Whitman."[60] As we can see, the construction, if there is one, is not only about mythologization or refusal; it is also about the dynamic variability of the elements that make up the figure of a successful author. As the title of the poetry book that Borges published in 1964 indicates, *The Other, the Same*. The hero is the other of the classical Borges of the 1960s and, consequently, he is the same.

CHAPTER 2

The Son at Work

It is possible that his faith is that of the Arians, who hold that the glory of the Son is a mere reflection of the glory of the Father.

"Story of the Warrior and the Captive Maiden," 1949[1]

An Unlikely Encounter in the Stairwell

If Borges's début into literature can be read in light of his heroic return to Buenos Aires in 1921, the passage from polemist tempted by nationalism and poet from the suburbs to great encyclopedic and speculative writer of the 1940s can be explained by another event: the accident he had in 1938 that almost cost him his life. At least, therein lies one of the versions that explains this change, as there exist in fact two different ways of telling the story of the evolution that would take place during the 1930s and that would lead to the production of three books, which, together, would ensure the celebrity of their author: two relatively short collections of short stories (*Ficciones* [*Fictions*] and *El Aleph*) and a collection of essays (*Otras inquisiciones, 19371952* [*Other Inquisitions*]).

There are therefore two explanatory versions. The first one highlights the textual operations, the abandonment of poetry, a lot of reading, and the successive approaches to short-story writing that emerge from the reviews and more or less imaginary biographies he wrote. The second one situates this choice within a personal mythology, which aimed, in itself, to render intelligible an enigmatic transformation by narrating it; by the same token, it ennobles the facts told in the sense that they produce extraordinary effects. It is quite significant indeed that this period of creativity and originality, the veritable result of many years of feeling the waters and learning, would conclude, in 1953, with his most important autobiographically inspired fiction, "The South." This story integrates the first public version of the accident and was, according to Borges, his "best" story:[2] is it surprising? As such, the period is framed on one end by a dramatic biographical adventure (illness and the confrontation with death), and on the other, by the story of this same anecdote as an explanation of the emergence of a different writer. "The South" functions as a kind of climax.

Let us begin with the accident and therefore with the myth. Michel Lafon presents the four main versions of the story; there are many more, sometimes two within the same book, juxtaposed for editorial purposes. Faced with this proliferation, Lafon attempts a functional study of the variants; other critiques, and they are many, have developed psychological or psychoanalytical interpretations. Here are the recurring elements in the story of the accident. The context is the period that follows the death of the writer's father. On Christmas Eve 1938, Borges has to pick up his wife at their house, he bolts up the stairs and runs into a window frame; in certain versions of the story the woman is "a very pretty young Chilean woman," maybe even the writer María Louisa Bombal; in others, no mention of the reason for Borges's being in the building is made; in some, he is running late and therefore is in a hurry; in others, the elevator is broken; and in the fictional version, "The South," he is rushing to consult "a copy (from which some pages were missing) of Weil's *Arabian Nights*."[3] He injures his head and it heals poorly, septicemia is declared, and neurological problems oblige an urgent surgical procedure; for some time, Borges is between life and death, suffering from high fever, nightmares, and painful insomnia. His convalescence is long, and Borges fears having lost his intellectual capacities during his illness. In one version, he says he tried to read *Mardi* by Herman Melville without managing to; in others, he asks his mother to read him something in English (apparently *Out of the Silent Planet* by C. S. Lewis) and bursts into tears when he is unable to understand the text. His fears were seemingly unfounded.

Up to now, I have tried to report the main components of the story, whose variations are significant and have justified the psychoanalytical interpretations made. Didier Anzieu draws a connection between the death of the father, the first family gathering at Christmas at which his mother was a widow, the attack on the brain (although Borges has hereditary loss of sight and his father died blind), and the presence of a desired woman, which allows for us to read in the accident, as he says, "unconscious mechanisms specific to faulty actions" and a close encounter with death that is close to a fantasy of punishment, derived from the tale of Oedipus.[4] Rodríguez Monegal sees it in a similar way and highlights that the accident freed Borges from the magisterium imposed by his father and from the guilt Borges felt after his father's death.[5]

Regardless, the plot that goes from the death of the father to his symbolic presence in the English language book read by his mother (English was associated with the paternal side of the family), not to mention the ordeal bringing on helplessness and danger, offers an image of Borges in a filial position. There is no child Borges (like Athena, little Georgie, according to his autobiography, possessed since his birth the traits of a writer in the making); however, there is a Borges son. Indeed, the few childhood memories that he recounts are literary and emphasize his multilingualism and general precocity: before the age of nine, he had written a manual of Greek mythology, read *Don Quixote* in English, and published a translation of Oscar Wilde, all without the help of his father who claimed "children educate their parents, not the other way around."[6]

In this sense, the noteworthy event of his childhood is without a doubt the mission he was given: the son of a part-time writer, Georgie had to become a writer in place of his father and one day correct the only novel published by Jorge Borges: "I was expected to become a writer."[7] The figure of the rewriter, which Lafon explores in depth in his book, might find its roots here as Borges seems to be destined to rewrite the work of his father. The ability to write or not sends us to his familial role, to this dilemma without an apparent solution between originality and the appropriation of what has already been written by an elder.

Setting aside the predictable dimension of the Oedipal crisis of a son confronted with the death of his father, what counts in the story of the accident is its strange unfolding. According to Borges—all the versions coincide on this point—this fear of losing his cognitive capacities then became a fear of being unable to continue his writerly activities. In order to face this fear and to diminish it, his response was to take on something new, for if he were to continue to practice the same genres (poetry, literary criticism, essays), the mental degradation provoked by the accident would have been visible. I will cite two versions of this development: "I wrote a story, telling myself that if I failed at the experiment, it wouldn't matter since it would only concern a genre within which I had never done anything before."[8] However, "if I tried something I had never really done before and failed at that it wouldn't be so bad and might even prepare me for the final revelation."[9] The story he would write is "Pierre Menard, Author of the Quixote,"[10] without a doubt one of the most significant of Borges's texts, as well as being the first in a series that, after a few intermedial publications, would take a nearly definitive form in 1944 under the title *Ficciones*: one of the most influential works of the twentieth century.

But if we take into consideration Borges's literary practices of the 1930s, and therefore the second version of his transition to prose stories, it appears that his development is fallacious and that its value is purely legendary: the proximity to death imposed by change establishes a connection between resurrection and the birth of writing. Through this story, which is in all likelihood unfounded, Borges invites us not to stop at his production predating 1939; in designating "Pierre Menard" as "something new, something important,"[11] he introduces a breaking point between the errors of his youth and the writer who, thanks to a borderline experience, would find his ultimate voice. In any case, according to Rodríguez Monegal, Borges became a different author, the author of "fascinating verbal labyrinths" and creator of a hybrid new form, between the story and the essay. He therefore positions himself above and beyond any of his father's plans.[12]

In any event, let us be reminded that this story began to be told in 1953, fifteen years after the accident, when Borges had already written and published three important books. The historical distance gives an impression of "after the fact" to the retrospective story, an impression of rearranging the past with regard for the "present" of a writing style. In this respect, it can be compared to the nonrepublication or to the corrections of the texts of his youth discussed in the previous chapter.

The 1930s: A Black Box

In his *Autobiographical Essay*, another version of the story of Borges's changes during the 1930s precedes, by a few pages, the story of the 1938 accident that we just discussed. In this essay he goes back over the beginning and the conditions of the emergence of his mature writing. Before arriving at the circumstances of the creation of "Pierre Menard," he refers to three important stages of his "entry into narration," just as there was before that an "entry into literature" thanks to the discovery of Buenos Aires and to his meeting Macedonio. I am going quite quickly through the 1930s not only to show the constructed nature of the story of the accident, but especially in order to shed light on these years, which are both mysterious and fundamental to Borges's trajectory.

The first milestone is the writing and rewriting of the story of a knife duel between scoundrels. Borges wrote the initial version, "Hombres pelearon" (Men fought),[13] which is more of a scene than an actual story, in secret, convinced that his mother "would highly disapprove of the subject matter," and more generally, of his writing a "suburban" story.[14] Despite this self-censorship, the text would be republished in the literary supplement of the magazine *Crítica* under a penname and with some corrections, "out of shyness, or perhaps a feeling that the story was a bit beneath me."[15] Eight years later the text would become "Hombre de la esquina rosada," ("Man on Pink Corner,") a well-structured story that was first published in 1933 then included two years later in *Historia universal de la infamia* (*A Universal History of Iniquity*[16]). The plot still focuses on the duel but has an added Oedipal dimension that would become obvious in other later rewritings, as Anzieu points out (for example "The Dead Man," a story included in *The Aleph*, 1949[17]). Borges indicates that "Man on Pink Corner" was his "first outright short story," all the while making sure to distinguish it from his later texts: "Although the story became popular to the point of embarrassment [. . .], I never regarded it as a starting point."[18] Nonetheless, the knife duel in question would be given a future in his stories to come (for example, "The End" and "The South," stories included in *Ficciones*); furthermore, as we can see, the starting point is arbitrary, merely the result of a decision ("I never regarded it [. . .]").

"The real beginning of my career as a story writer starts with the series of sketches entitled *Historia universal de la infamia*," he says, in a statement that reveals his insistent quest for "beginnings."[19] This 1935 work can therefore be considered the second milestone. The book brings together a series of somewhat true biographies of "infamous" characters, following a model strongly influenced by Marcel Schwob's *Imaginary Lives* (and more generally by the English tradition of short biographies). The stories were first published in a widely circulated literary supplement managed by Borges, the *Revista multicolor de los Sábados*, and were not originally intended to become a book. In this instance as well, it seems as though fictional writing was not accepted or was perceived as somewhat of a lesser or even raffish activity; in the preface to the 1954 edition, he would say that these stories were "the irresponsible sport of a shy sort of man who could not bring himself to write short stories, and so amused himself by changing and distorting (sometimes without any aesthetic justification) the stories of other men."[20]

Despite the self-critique—in the same preface—of the baroque style of his prose of the time, *A Universal History* already contains elements of storytelling done through rewriting, the pseudo-essay, imaginary bibliographic references, and the narrative pattern of biography, elements that are obvious precursory signs pointing to the great stories of the 1940s. The same thing could be said about the belief in reading as a practice equivalent to writing, an idea he puts forth in the preface of the first edition of *A Universal History*: "I sometimes think that good readers are poets as singular, and as awesome, as great authors themselves," and further on, "Reading, meanwhile, is an activity subsequent to writing—more resigned, more civil, more intellectual." This is a defense of the function and perhaps of the rights of him or her who arrives after, the reader—and why not, of the son, but I'll come back to that. In the end, it must be noted that in light of so much reticence or apparent self-censorship, the title is an ironic and messianic hyperbole; we are talking about a *universal* story, nothing less, and "Man on Pink Corner" incarnates the Argentine avatar of infamy. Borges inscribes his characters in a universal history, but he does it through a history of the slums and of infamy. The margins, the *orillas*, are always at work in his writing; ambition can always be found behind reticence.

"The Approach to Al-Mu'tasim," which was published for the first time in 1936 in *Historia de la eternidad* (A history of eternity; a book of essays), was, as Borges said, both a "hoax *and* a pseudo-essay."[21] The story presents itself as the summary of an invented book, written by an imaginary author, even if the editor and the author of the preface are real. Here we find the first example of the use of the essay as well as the format of the bibliographical sheet, contextualization in a distant cultural sphere (the fictitious book is set in India and includes erudite references to Muslim mysticism), and above all the decision to provide commentary on nonexistent books as a writing device. This may be why Borges considers, again in his *Autobiographical Essay*, that this story "foreshadow[s]" and even "set[s] the pattern for those tales that were somehow awaiting me, and upon which my reputation as a storyteller was to be based."[22] As proof, "The Approach to Al-Mu'tasim" was included in the different editions of *Ficciones* until 1974 when, in the edition of the *Obras completas* (in Spanish), it was reinserted in its original context of publication, *Historia de la eternidad*, relegating it to the exclusive function of precursory text to "Pierre Menard."

Borges was not afraid to provide diverging explanations. On the one hand, he followed the steps leading up to storytelling, which contained many heralding hints and gradual approaches. This staging of a slow and progressive emergence of stories tends to emphasize the importance of the texts to come, since they justify such a detailed path. On the other hand, in the same book, he offers a second version, that of the 1938 accident, haloed with the mythical aspect surrounding change following a major vital crisis; with this gesture, he reinforces difference, emphasizes mutation, and instills a break where continuity was apparent. Indeed, as much from the point of view of genres (a structured story) as from that of the practice of narration that appropriates certain established forms of essays (summaries, obituaries, literary biographies), "Pierre Menard" is in no way a novelty; rather, it emerges as a bibliographical false note, as do "The Approach to Al-Mu'tasim" and other preceding texts.

Simultaneously, and to complement the coordinates of the "black box" that the 1930s represented for him (he enters it with his last book on an "Argentine" subject, *Evaristo Carriego*, and exits it with a noteworthy encyclopedic fable), Borges was quite disappointed by the lack of repercussions produced by the writing of his youth, as Rodríguez Monegal reminds us, most of all, by the limited reception of his three poetry books (he was confronted with the obvious fact that he would not become the "Argentine Whitman," as he had dreamt at the time; he would not therefore become "a wide-reaching cosmic poet."[23] The same then went for his attempt to expand on "Argentine" subjects: *Evaristo Carriego* was a failure, and included in the failure, was the baroque style of the book. An even more powerful example: when it first came out, *Historia de la eternidad* only sold thirty-seven copies.

The crisis, if there was one, took place not only in a stairwell in 1938, it spanned an entire decade during which Borges sought to make a path for the literary destiny that at the time seemed to escape him. In 1934 he even attempted suicide, an episode that was concealed from his biography until his old age, when he was confronted with his imminent death; he would then incorporate it in a late short story ("August 25, 1983,") in which he repeats the gesture of autobiographical fabulation adopted in "The South." In any case, in a poem written in old age ("The Past"), he would revisit the ambitions of Whitman, which can help clarify those of Borges at the time: "Whitman, who in his Brooklyn office / amidst the smell of ink and tobacco / becomes, and says nothing of, this infinity / resolves to be all men / and to write the book that is them all."[24]

In any event, if Borges would develop a feverish activity during the 1930s, his writing would not only be of a creative nature. At that point, poetry had taken on a subaltern role; in the decades to come, he would publish editions of his poems on several occasions, always including his early poems, with many corrections, as well as a handful of texts written after 1929, when *Cuaderno San Martín* (*Poemas 1922–1943*, *Poemas 1923–1953*, etc.) would come out. It was only in 1960 (*El hacedor* [*The Maker*]) and in more notably in 1964 (*El otro, el mismo* [The other, the same / *The Self and the Other*]) that the poetic production from his mature years would find autonomous editorial visibility.

In the 1930s, except for the "narrative exercises" of *A Universal History of Iniquity* and the procrastination surrounding the first story, his writing focused on the essay, in the largest sense of the term. Let us note the publication of two works in which the philosophical inspiration and premises on the fertility of metaphysics for the imagination are apparent, along with the deployment of a somewhat brazen erudition. With *A History of Eternity* (1936), on the one hand, we have a book whose title is in itself an agenda for the "new" Borges, as it presents a paradox: eternity, if it exists, could not have a history, or therefore any inscription in chronological time. On the other hand, we have *Discusión* (*Discussion*; 1932), an important book for the evolution of the writer. He extends his interest in the "Argentine essence" and in the texts that might represent it (in particular the *gauchesca* literature), as well as his writing in the margins of metaphysics. But most importantly several essays directly take on questions of narration, a bit like certain texts on poetic writing from the previous decade. Whether it be on the reader, on the ways to represent the real, or on causality in the novel, *Discussion* offers reflections that would be read abundantly, as a counterpoint to Borges's great stories. It must then be noted that of all the essays dedicated to writers, those on novelists dominate (he included two articles on Flaubert in particular). During the same period, he produced and published summaries of contemporary novels and short biographies of authors of his time in a substantial number of journals.

It was through writing essays and reading novels—not through poetry—that Borges would seek his literary future, his tone, his path. He thought a lot about the format of the story before beginning to actually write stories; he theorized on the position of the reader; he analyzed the narrative production of his time (in integrating minor genres such as adventure novels, police novels, and Hollywood films). Borges's "glorious decade" (the 1940s) emerges as a highpoint after years of reorienting his literary career, learning how to write stories, and constructing an alternative identity to prophetic heroism: the identity of a son as a writer of stories.

Writing the Quixote

Let us now return to "Pierre Menard." The story presents itself as a bio-bibliographic note on a writer from Nîmes who has recently died; the narrator, a friend of the author, first details the "visible" bibliography, a parodic catalogue of a pretentious man of letters of minor importance. Then he takes on the task of describing the other side of Menard's creation, the "invisible work," an ambitious project that turns him into a kind of misunderstood writer: a new writing of the *Quixote*, the greatest literary classic in the Spanish language. The conditions he imposed on himself for this task, although implausible, are explained in detail: he did not want to "rewrite" the Quixote, nor to merely "copy" it, or even less to "be" Cervantes by appropriating—through identification, of doubtful viability—his tastes, culture, or world view. His objective was to write the Quixote again, all the while remaining who he was, a French writer from Nîmes, a town far from Spanish literature. "To be a popular novelist of the seventeenth century in the twentieth seemed to Menard to be a diminution"; "continuing to be Pierre Menard and coming to the Quixote *through the experiences of Pierre Menard.*"[25] This is the meaning of the title of the story, turning Menard into the author of the *Quixote*.

It is therefore neither a matter, for him, of adapting the classic to contemporary times, nor of returning to the moment of its creation, but of erasing, in a way, the historicity of the text to reveal the possibility of writing a book that would coincide "word for word and line for line" (91) with that of Cervantes. The task is tough, more arduous than it was for the Spaniard: "My obliging predecessor did not spurn the collaboration of chance; his method of composition for the immortal book was a bit *à la diable*, [...] I have assumed the mysterious obligation to reconstruct, word for word, the novel that for him was spontaneous" (92–93). After the description of the project, the narrator compares passages of the two texts—identical, of course—and analyses the differences in meaning between the seventeenth-century version and the contemporary text; the historical displacement significantly modifies the reading of the *Quixote*. An evaluation of the meaning of this paradoxical work and of its reach closes out the story.

"Pierre Menard" is above all an elaborate hoax invented to force the redefinition of our conceptions of influence, literary history, rewriting, and originality; the insolent, derisive tone of Borges's youth can be found in this text that in the end reads as a kind of joke, full of humorous references and ironic statements. Menard's position before Cervantes is provocative, or even iconoclastic: the classic book does not occupy a specific place, it is not a monument; it is merely an item we can work with to manage to write our own personal works. In fact, Menard says that he has merely a vague memory of his model: "My general recollection of the Quixote, simplified by forgetfulness and indifference, might well be the equivalent of the vague foreshadowing of a yet unwritten book" (92). We are not far from iconoclasm here. And this is no exception; in Borges's work, writing often leads to a process of endangering conventional forms of thought and epistemological paradigms. Rewriting is never a reverential reproduction.[26]

The story also develops an unconventional modality of the fantastic, in the sense that it suggests an implosion of reason, not through the apparition of a supernatural being or the questioning of the coordinates of identity, time, or space that govern our world, but through the description of an impossible thing presented as natural and intelligible: how can we conceive of this writing that is neither copy, nor remake, nor adaptation? Considering Menard's project as rational requires breaking with the way we think about and understand our world. "The stark impossibility of thinking *that*," remarked Foucault about another of Borges's texts.[27] The effect is of that nature. Just as in Kafka's *The Metamorphosis*, the main narrative of the plot is infinitely suggestive and highly enigmatic.

Moreover, to the extent that the text appears to be a bibliographic commentary containing a eulogy, or perhaps a scholarly summary, the heart of the plot lies in this inconceivable composition and this incomprehensible project. It turns out that the invention taking place in the story is more related to the identity, the role, and the objectives of an author than it is to fitting the plot into a traditional narrative form. The story here is the author and a bibliography. In this sense, the story amplifies what takes place with "The Approach to Al-Mu'tasim," imagining an unwritten book, imagining a nonexistent author, and building around them a text that borrows its codes from the essay. Beyond the deceptive inventiveness of the formal aspects of the story, proclaimed through the story of the accident, we can say that change, rupture, and novelty are found especially in the imaginary creation of a writer executing an inconceivable task. Already, in *Evaristo Carriego*, Borges had sketched out a narrative based on the biography of a writer, and in "The Approach to Al-Mu'tasim," proposed a commentary of a nonexistent book. In the 1939 story, he goes one step further. Literary creation becomes for the author a fabulation in which he can represent himself as other; such was the prerequisite condition to writing fiction. This is not the romantic *topos* of life perceived as a work of art, but rather an act of imagining lives and different authorial identities as a form of literary creation.

Borges sees himself here as an unrecognized author, incapable of originality, condemned to failure, enslaved to impossible tasks. With that in mind, the story of the 1938 accident, as it explains in legendary terms the writing of this text, puts a limit on the heroism of his youth; the confrontation with the dead father, with literary figures of reference (in this case, Cervantes), and with the codes of tradition update, in Borges, an Oedipal aporia (you must be like your father but you do not have the right to be equal to him). To sum it up: the death of the father and the experience with death justify the sudden turn to radical originality and to novelty that would completely change Borges's writing. However, the result, the originality, and the novelty lie in the creation of a text on impossible originality, on rewriting as novelty, and on repetition as a plan for creation. The accident seems, by way of Menard, to give a new face to Borges, the author in search of a work and of recognition: the face of a son before an unsolvable equation.

A Position on Culture

This authorial fiction, in deploying aporias and the contemporaneity of contradictory events, seeks to eliminate the imperative nature of literary filiations by undermining the role of classics and of heritage. If the writer, for Borges, is he who comes after—the original is always the other[28]—and if the writer's role is that of the son, the story highlights the possibility of writing despite the overwhelming library inherited. This is one of the facets of the modern position of creators: on the one hand, we find a messianism surrounding innovation, and on the other, a pessimistic clarity on the potential continuity of art. Or, more precisely, the question is: how does one write a "classic" work in Argentina in the 1930s? Composing the *Quixote* "in the early seventeenth century was a reasonable, necessary, and perhaps even inevitable enterprise; in the early twentieth century, it is virtually impossible" (Pierre Menard," 93). This conclusion led Borges to invent a new authorial position, that of Pierre Menard, a marginal writer who enjoys going for walks "in the evening," "on the outskirts of Nîmes" (95), like Borges in the *orillas* of Buenos Aires; in this way, the author accomplishes a titanic task: "repeating in a foreign tongue a book that already existed" (95).

It is no longer a matter of being the first, but of arriving after and traveling through the monuments of literature; it might even be a matter of being the last one—in the historical sequence or within a geographical location—in order to become, despite everything, the first. Therefore, without occupying the role of the master Cervantes, without ceasing to be a marginal, provincial author lacking visibility, Menard manages to write the Great Text again, as if it had never been written, and even to write it "better." The myth inverts the order of creation: any writer can write a classic; anyone, in fact, can write a classic (even a son whose father just passed away, even an Argentine, even Borges who, in writing this story wrote his first "classic.") The author, with unambiguous modesty, makes possible the emergence of a transformational work. Confronted with the paternal sphere as a figure (Cervantes), as a text (the *Quixote*) and as an inherited code of a tradition (a language and culture imposed), the position allows him both to express an ambition and to carry out the paternal mandate: to become a writer in lieu of his father, and to be a better writer than the father, all the while rendering a paradoxical cult book in which figures of reference are on the verge of dethronement. In any case, the desire to write a "classic" that might withstand time and that might find its place among the ranks of other great monuments in literary history is explicit, despite the repeated denial and the rhetorical devices giving an impression of modesty.

In any case, it is now understood that, in addition to the imaginary or the subconscious aspects of this episode, the renewal of a literary project is at stake in "Pierre Menard." Many affirmative statements serving to advance an agenda can be found in the plot before the story concludes with a final learned anecdote. For example, there is an insolent and prophetic statement in favor of intellectual power: "Every man should be capable of all ideas, and I believe that in the future he shall be" (95). Another statement reminds us of the inevitable transformation of philosophical systems that, with time, cease to be "a plausible description of the universe" (94) and are instead reduced to a line or a name in the history of philosophy (or of literature). But without a doubt, the most important sentence in "Pierre Menard" is the proclamation of a "new" writing "technique": "the technique of deliberate anachronism and fallacious attribution" (95). The novelty resides in the cancellation of a stable authorial identity (to write, one conducts "fallacious attributions") and in the ability, through anachronism, to reduce the fatality that determines the succession of authors and works in an inevitable chronological line, as occurs with the succession of generations from fathers to sons.

In terms of projection toward a work to come, a comparison can be established between the insolent ambition of this story and that of another written the following year, "Tlön, Uqbar, Orbis Tertius," which opens all the editions of *Ficciones*. The main issue in the story is the invention of a virtual world (a Tlön world whose apocryphal encyclopedia is discovered by chance), a world made up of deformed but recognizable elements from our world (its history, metaphysics, literature, and art).

At the climax of the story, we learn that this parallel world will soon replace ours, that is, 1930s Europe dominated by totalitarianism. This alternate universe, in addition to the historical perspective it provides, also serves as a catalogue of the literary world that Borges would begin to write in the 1940s: in one way or another, all his stories, aesthetic concerns, rhetorical devices, tastes, and obsessions can already be detected.

If in his early poetry books Borges was inventing a city, Buenos Aires, on the threshold of his first book of short stories, produced in his mature years, he announces, like a demiurge, the cosmos that would be born from his pen over the next ten years. After seeing himself as a son who rewrites, he delimits a nonexistent world, even before filling it with characters, plots, or ideas. "Pierre Menard" is a paradoxical tool that allowed him to go from the "irresponsible sport of a shy sort of man who could not bring himself to write short stories" to the messianism apparent in the conception of Tlön, this "illusory world" sufficiently powerful to intrude into the real world, by substituting its "harmonious history" for a "fictitious past," as we can read in the final pages of the story.[29] Finally, we should point out the continuity, despite the visible ruptures: this "fictitious past" invented by Borges is a late echo of an "illusory past" that men and women would be able to share after the "mythological founding of Buenos Aires" in the 1926 eponymous poem.[30]

A Narcissistic Utopia

In "Literary Utopia" (1966), a significant text for the international reception of Borges, Gérard Genette analyzes certain aspects of the singular position of the author before literature, in particular the principle that leads him to believe that "the time of a work is not the defined time of writing, but the indefinite time of reading and of memory." Literature, as such, is seen as a gigantic textual corpus within which works respond to each other in "a homogenous and reversible space where individual particularities and chronological details do not rule the day." Genette calls this vision a myth (in other words "a deep-seated intention of thought") as well as a "totalitarian utopia," which questions the preconceived idea that "a work is essentially determined by its author, and consequently, *expresses* the author."[31] Yet Borges would defend the idea of the "entirely literary," according to which chronology and familial ties between the author to his work are null; accordingly, in this space where everything is already written, Kafka has as much influence on Cervantes as Cervantes does on Kafka. Literature is precisely this plastic field, this *curved* space in which the most unexpected relationships and the most paradoxical encounters are possible at every instant.

As we can see, Genette reads in Borges what would become the great theoretical concerns of the 1960s in France: questioning the author and the intertextual value of all writing (a few years later, Genette himself would publish a book on the matter, *Palimpsests* [1982], in which he would extend his reading of the Argentine whose story already contained the word "palimpsest," using it to describe the connections between Cervantes's text and Menard's). He sees in Borges a claim in favor of the autonomy of the meaning of works with regard to the context of production and to the internationalities of their authors. Menard, in that respect, is the legendary figure that serves to express a certain way of reading, reading taking on a value equivalent if not superior to writing. Naturally, we are here at the heart of a unique conception of literature that would have multiple ramifications in Borges's work, certain of which will be discussed later on, in particular the vision of literary history, the function of precursors and the notion of influence.

For the moment and with the point of view developed here, I would say that the reader, for Borges in 1939, is above all the one who arrives after, when all is done, all is written, who can merely stroll through the monuments of the past—as a counterpoint to the belief in heroic foundation. In this sense, the reader can be seen as a filial figure. Borges, in "Pierre Menard," transforms negativity into creativity and exposes the proverbial weakness of modern writing, turning it into the basis for redefined innovation. The son can continue to write because it is in repetition that one finds originality; novelty, from that point on, is the *Quixote*. In spite of the insurmountable barriers between generations and the inevitability of time, it is possible for a current author to rise to the ranks of the great figures of literary history who can be rewritten, just as new fantasies can be built that erase differences and presume virtual equivalence between all writers of the past and present.

Without a doubt, the utopia of a literature free from names of authors and circumstances of production, a utopia shrouded in the trappings of modesty, is attractive. However, we can clearly recognize a narcissistic posture behind it. Anzieu sees in narcissism the content of Borges's work itself as it introduces an inventory "of its figures, its beliefs, its typical ways of reasoning,"[32] such as fascination with the specular image (the double, the reflection, the echo, inverse symmetry, the horrors of mirrors) or with the circle (that turns round and round itself and desires to be the center of the world). The same goes for certain statements that characterize Borges's work in a similar way: in order for one to live the other must die; one man is all men; there is a place that contains all other places; differences tend to be denied. It also goes for certain ideals: creating a new language; building new societies, new worlds; gathering in a single library all the books ever written and to be written; escaping generation and the sexual act in order to engender himself.[33] If all men are a single man and if they are no one, including canonical authors, the filial position also contains a narcissistic dimension; I can be Cervantes (and in other texts, I can be Homer or Shakespeare); I can be all of the great men of history, but the great men of history are, as for themselves, no one.

Thus ambivalence dominates. The writer who denies his or her originality, who submits to repetition as an essential paradigm of creation, who constantly reveres his or her elders, who presents him or herself as a librarian or an infinite reader, who rejects the idea of a given, stable tradition, is the writer who manages to place him or herself at the heart of a new tradition. Borges turns a personal (biographical, fantastic) anecdote into an important cultural issue. Impossible originality, the "all is written," the disenchanted self-reflexive vision of twentieth-century writers, the ways they place themselves in a world saturated with signs and traditions, are engrained in a personal destiny, in a filial position, which is why the figure of the son, thanks to the his personal myth, is much more than a familial image or a print left by an Oedipal fantasy; it is a symbolic structure allowing the author to situate himself in cultural history.

Borges updates the legendary values of confrontations between masters and disciples found in literary history, going from a period of generational opposition and parricidal attacks to a much more complex, effective, and nuanced system. Pierre Menard is a figure that tells us of the aporias of modern literature and raises the questions of influence, intertextuality, and originality, all the while transforming them. It goes beyond the adventures taking place in the story and embodies much more than mere Borgesian self-representation; in that respect, Menard is like Kafka's K. Creating such figures is without a doubt the mark of a great writer. Borges, as a son, has finally emerged.

The Years of Expansion

In the span of a few years, Borges wrote the great stories and essays that contributed to his singularity. It is undeniable that with "Pierre Menard" his creativity was liberated, allowing for many significant texts to emerge in little time. In December 1941, the first part of what would later become *Ficciones* was published under the title of one of the eight stories included in the book, *El jardín de senderos que se bifurcan* (*The Garden of Forking Paths*). A second part, *Artificios* (*Artifices*), would be added to the 1944 edition of the book; and Borges would add three more texts (including "The South") to the 1956 edition. Starting in 1944, Borges would compose a second series of stories, grouped together in 1949 under the title *The Aleph*, a collection to which he would add five stories when it was reedited in 1952. Simultaneously (both in terms of writing periods and in terms of a similar way of making literature), he would begin in 1939 to publish short essays (especially for the magazine *Sur* headed by Victoria Ocampo), which would form a collection published in 1952, *Other Inquisitions* (about forty texts that also contain variations between editions and republications).

These are unbelievably dense texts, overloaded with logical operations, interconnected scholarly references, and delayed semantic effects. In this respect, if there is no novel in Borges, there is nevertheless a sophisticated construction that goes largely beyond each story or essay; there is a unique system structured by obsessions: tigers, mirrors, labyrinths, duels, the double, memory, the dream, the existence of magical or supernatural words, infinity and temporal alterations, and so on. A coherent series of processes, references, and rewritings compensates for the fragmentation of ideas into short texts; a tightly knit thread of recurrent names, self-quotations, and other twists completes this effect. The whole thing, monumental in its own way, defines the shape of a body of work to come. The conception that determines the functioning and the semantic circulation of his texts appears to be that which Borges summed up in 1951 when he wrote, "literature is not exhaustible, for the sufficient and simple reason that a single book is not. A book is not an isolated entity: it is a narration, an axis of innumerable narrations."[34]

In these books, we therefore find the most well-known and the most commented on characteristics of his work and the texts that form the "core" of his literary personality. First of all, an insolent, exasperated, exacerbated erudition that is not far from the idea of encyclopedic totality: the entire library is put to the service of these fabulations, which is why the entire library must be read in order to understand them. These scholarly storylines are often nourished by theology, philosophy ("metaphysics is a branch of the literature of fantasy," as the metaphysicians of Tlön believe,[35] while Borges sees himself as "an Argentine adrift on a sea of metaphysics"[36]), and even by mathematics. Nonetheless a continuous line of "typically Argentine" texts is continued: the pampa of the nineteenth century, the slums, the knife duels. Furthermore, after the *Quixote*, Borges takes on another classic, of Argentine literature this time, and writes a story that prolongs *Martín Fierro* (1872–1879) by José Hernández and another that provides side information on one of its characters ("The End" in *Ficciones* and "A Biography of Tadeo Isidoro Cruz [1829–1874] in *The Aleph*).

Despite modest formulas and discrete engagements, the Borgesian imagination of the time was built around messianic textual artefacts that challenge the limitations of human beings and question the intelligibility of the universe: parallel worlds, sacred objects, magical completeness, words borrowed from the language of the divine. Elsewhere, greatness and strangeness settle into the unusual, imaginary, unbelievable, and highly metaphorical or symbolic places and structures: the labyrinth of Crete, in which "each part of the house occurs many times; any particular place is another place" ("The House of Asterion,"[37]); the immense spherical prison of "The Writing of God"; the Library of Babel, which equates to the universe; the garden of forking paths, this image of time incessantly diverging. On certain occasions, it is the book itself that becomes a space of invention (a fictional encyclopedia is at the heart of "Tlön, Uqbar, Orbis Tertius"; virtual works and works that are impossible to write appear in "The Secret Miracle" and "A Survey of the Works of Herbert Quain"). The repetitions, obsessions, and artefacts surrounding his biography, just as much as the legendary stories, would ensure his significant symbolic presence in literary history.

The Prestige of Melancholy

The illicit founder that is Menard, just like the other distorted self-representations of Borges, would long be embodied in the works to come. The one that appears in another "classic" story, "The Library of Babel" (*Ficciones*), can serve to complement the rewriter from Nîmes as a character. The story picks up on an essay published three months after "Pierre Menard," "The Total Library" (August 1939).

In the essay, Borges develops of kind of utopia, that of a library that might combine everything that has been written and everything that humans might one day write, by presenting us with a certain number of authors from the past who have imagined this completeness, often obtained through a combinatory approach to the letters of the alphabet. The result is inconceivable: by playing with letters, we can manufacture an incredible number of books; the supposed content of this fictitious library, quite similar to that of "The Library of Babel," is described through vertiginous enumeration: "Everything would be in its blind volumes. Everything: the detailed history of the future, Aeschylus' *The Egyptians*, the exact number of times that the waters of the Ganges have reflected the flight of a falcon, the secret and true name of Rome, the encyclopedia Novalis would have constructed, my dreams and half-dreams at dawn on August 14, 1934,"[38] and so on. In "The Library of Babel" we read: "*All*—the detailed history of the future, the autobiographies of the archangels, the faithful catalog of the Library, thousands and thousands of false catalogs, the proof of the falsity of those false catalogs, a proof of the falsity of the *true* catalog," and even "the true story of your death, the translation of every book into every language, the interpolations of every book into all books,"[39] and so on.

Two radical differences exist, nonetheless, between the essay and the story: the utopia of "The Total Library" takes on the form of a Kafka-inspired nightmare in "The Library of Babel," and in this second Library, there is someone, a librarian, an ailing person, while the first Library is empty. The story places a subject in the form of an exaggerated self-portrait before the speculations surrounding a combinatory of signs and a calculation of possibilities. This character, the librarian, is not only the son who has arrived too late; he is also someone who finds himself in the imagined emotional position known as melancholy. Borges said, in one of his frequent commentaries offering retrospective explanations of his stories, that he presented two "ideas" in "The Library of Babel."

The first is the "possibility of nearly infinite variation beginning with a limited number of elements," a "quite old" abstract idea that leads to another, highlighting the fact that "words—and consequently ideas—are but combinations of letters," which corresponds to a strictly formalist and mathematical vision of language. The second idea is not really an idea; it is an intention to transform the combinatory into a nightmare, by accounting for a feeling: that of being "lost in the universe, of not understanding, the desire to find a specific answer, the feeling of not knowing the true answer."[40] On the one hand, an abstract perception of language, on the other, an imaginary melancholic burden perceivable in the image of a subject lost in an irrevocably hermetic world. This double-sided motivation (an idea and an emotion) is in all aspects emblematic of Borges's literary practice and must constantly be taken into account when approaching his texts. First, thought, logic, and intelligence are at work, then disorientation or shock engages the realm of emotions.

The duality of the initial project is discernable in the published story. We read of the development of an exhaustive geometric form (a hexagon) that structures the library and that, through repetition, devises a labyrinth without a center and without exits, an exacerbated image of enclosure. Coherent, regular, and monotonous, the Library repeats its hexagons, which suggest infinity (as much in space as in time) as well as a strict, logical version of chaos. This shifting of intelligence toward the limits of reason—a repeated geometric form that leads to bewilderment—is characteristic of the fantastic in Borges. In this universe there is no other reality than books, and their arrangement is an arbitrary order: identical shelves go on without any other physical, biological, or imagined reality. Books neither represent nor say anything, for there is only one code emptied of all substance. Writing, a system of signs, is the one sphere of existence possible, and it replaces, in a spectacular reversal, all autonomous referents. The Library and the universe are one and the same. The image, dear to Borges, of the primacy of writing over the real finds here its most extreme version: there is no reality, and writing is but a form, as aberrant as it is totalitarian.

Identical volumes in the Library therefore contain texts determined by chance through the combination of twenty-six letters of the alphabet. Their number, if we take into account an average number of characters per line, lines per page, and pages per book, would be $25^{1,320,000}$ according to a mathematician's calculation: a number that is not infinite, but is unbelievable, that renders practically inexistent the books actually written and published since humans began to think and create.[41] Here too, we observe a drastic elusion of experience, intention, communication, and even intelligence; only chance governs expression (in "The Total Library," there is even a delirious God and texts that eliminate intelligence[42]). Writing can only be involuntary repetition; originality is banned until the end of time. Contrary to the divine word of cosmogonies or the word inspired by poets, language is altered by the hyperbolic exacerbation of its characteristics: the combination of its elementary components, letters. This is clearly nightmarish, but the nightmare is that of the son in his role of librarian. A crisis of representation is no longer denoted; instead, we have images of a cataclysm of representation, of a logical collapse of language, and of a symmetrical and equilibrated apocalypse.

"The Library of Babel" also integrates a subject, a draft of a biography, a foretaste of a storyline. The story is told by a narrator-protagonist who develops a dynamic of and a tendency toward melancholy (complaint, nostalgia for meaning beyond reach, a quest for explanations about the universe, a painful consideration of the past, degradation, pessimism, the imminent presence of death).[43] This is not surprising, for the idea of a combination of elements leading to infinite multiplication is mentioned at the beginning of the story, through an epigraph taken from *The Anatomy of Melancholy* by Robert Burton ("By this art you may contemplate the variation of the 23 letters..."[44]) This seventeenth-century encyclopedic work, an emblem in itself of the failed quest for knowledge and meaning, therefore frames the story. The narrator, at the end of his existence, after a life searching for Order or Meaning in the labyrinth of the Library, is about to die—and, shortly after his death, the human race is also going to disappear, the humankind whose religious, ideological, and philosophical history is evoked in the story of the Library's past.

At the end of his life, the narrator, almost blind, latches on to a thread of hope, awaiting some kind of Order in the universe. Even if this hopefulness engenders a somewhat touching tone in the last sentence of the story, it is rather rhetorical: the only truth available— and it is a horrific truth—is the image of death, which, as early as the second paragraph, is presented to us at the same time as the spatial description of the Library. This is the future of the subject: "When I am dead, compassionate hands will throw me over the railing; my tomb will be the unfathomable air, my body will sink for ages, and will decay and dissolve in the wind engendered by my fall, which shall be infinite."[45] Infinite death, negative obsession that corresponds to the characteristics of the space, for how could we not see, in the lifeless landscape of the library, in this desert of darkness and repetition, a reproduction of the landscapes typical of melancholy? There is here a real "depressive unrealization."[46] The world has disappeared and what has replaced it is a dead world. With Burton in mind, Borges engendered an encyclopedic, melancholic, and terrifying situation.

The Pleasures of Loss

The key to this mechanism is the function of loss as a primitive experience that becomes an existential position for the writer. According to this experience, emptiness will find itself transformed into absence, into something that is no longer there, that has been lost. Borges's Buenos Aires was already a city permeated by loss; the radical newness and the epic foundation were completed through the perception of time painfully slipping away—each day, the city changes—in other words, a past time that we could not stop in order to possess in its entirety. The city it not only mythical, it is also associated with the past, a past created while it is evoked with foundational nostalgia.

The superimposition of heroic gesture and melancholic regret also emerge in many other aspects of the works. The stories in which the protagonist experiences omnipotence and attains cosmic wisdom are numerous: he learns the secret name of God; he manages to become immortal; he contemplates the entire universe from a supernatural perspective; he possesses a fantasy object. However, these approaches to the highly desired realm of the enchanted just as soon turn toward destruction ("The Aleph"), voluntary loss ("The Zahir"), or abandonment ("The Writing of the God"), or become a quest for basic mortal purpose ("The Immortal").

The result, melancholic and elegant, is always the same: now I am no one; I was and I am no longer; I am everything and I am nothing. The son exhibits limitless heroism and ambition, only to then integrate the law, natural or human, and cast a regretful gaze on the bygone past. To be everyone, to be everything and to be nothing, or perhaps to get a sense of absolute possession and wake up with empty hands; this is what is at stake. Fantasy is not foreign to the belief that "being nothing is more than being something and is, in some way, to be everything," an idea exposed and criticized in a text from *Other Inquisitions*, "From Someone to Nobody."[47] The negation of being and the lamentation that follows come with hidden satisfaction.

Melancholy, as Agamben suggests, implies lamenting the disappearance of something that was never possessed, but that, through this same lamentation, seems to have been possessed in the past.[48] As for Borges, he expresses the fantasized nature of loss by stating repeatedly, as in "A New Refutation of Time," "one loses only what one really never had."[49] Telling of the experimentations that allow one to reach an almost divine position only to then lose it, and exploiting the nostalgia for a Buenos Aires that was just created are mechanisms that imply the imaginary possession of what is out of man's reach.

In this respect, it is highly significant that the only two romantic experiences present (as memories rather than as passionate experiences) in the stories of the 1940s function in this way. Two beloved but deceased women appear in "The Aleph" and "The Zahir." In both cases, the death of the woman is quickly replaced by a magical empowering experience: discovering the Aleph, a perspective that allows one to simultaneously observe the totality of the world and of time, and finding the Zahir, a magical object, according to an imaginary Muslim tradition, that is, in Buenos Aires, a twenty-cent piece that can never be forgotten. But the Aleph gets destroyed and the Zahir is voluntarily misplaced in an attempt to escape its influence. Only when omnipotence has been attained can the lamentations over the deceased women be quelled. Lamenting over women, choosing the banality of human experience over heroic destiny, means both accepting that love will never be had and neither will superhuman qualities, all the while advancing the idea that this love did indeed exist and that superhuman power was once experienced. Melancholy, in a way, is not only a position that inscribed Borges within the noble tradition of representing a certain spirituality since Antiquity; it is also a means for him to invent his own extraordinary destiny, to fulfill his desires, and demonstrate his skills, both apparent and inconceivable.

Consolation for loss is therefore found through a paradoxical messianism. In one of the few instances of Borges's work dedicated to the subject of "love," two sonnets published together titled "1964," Borges makes reference to an unforgettable abandonment ("But, to learn the fine art of forgetting, / it is not enough to put on a brave face"), an abandonment that impoverishes the world ("It is not magic now, the world. Alone"). However, consolation arrives: "We only lose (you vainly tell yourself) / what we do not have, what we have never had." Loss might, in the end, be a retrospective mode of possession and bewilderment before the world leading to consolation: "I will not be happy now. It may not matter. / There are so many more things in the world. / Any random instant is as crowded / and varied as the sea."[50]

Loss, lamentation, exceptionality, attraction to a bygone past, paradoxical lucidity, superhuman worlds bereft of life, moments of bitter reflection on oneself and on the world, pessimism, erudition, nostalgia for untraceable meaning: these are some of the characteristics typical of melancholy accentuated in Borges's work. A form of melancholy that can be considered as a highly coded cultural image inseparable, since the Renaissance at least, from the idea that poets create their own conditions.[51]

Coming back to "The Library of Babel" and to conclude on this point, let us say that on the one hand, we have splendid invention—"The Universe (which others call the Library)" is the extraordinary opening to this story[52]—and on the other hand, we can highlight everything that escapes this apparently all-powerful writer. After his foundational youth of the 1920s, the author becomes a dead man

(Menard) or an aging, skeptical librarian, overwhelmed by an undefined loss, in mourning over a nonexistent object that might be, in accordance with Freud, the essence of melancholy.[53]

In any case, pessimistic lucidity would dominate in Borges's self-representations from the 1940s on. It is in these kinds of situations that we see him, in the climax of "Tlön, Uqbar, Orbis Tertius" for example, trapped in a useless translation, neglecting the end of the world. He also appears this way in the preface to the second edition of *Evaristo Carriego*, as a recluse in the father's library full of countless books in English. In the "Poem of the Gifts," twenty years later, he wanders through the long corridors of the Argentine National Library, a tall and deep library that he manages, mumbling: "I am that other dead one, who attempted / the same uncertain steps on similar days."[54] This is how he would appear in the countless iconographies of his old age. At forty, Borges was not only a writer capable of inventing worlds and rewriting the great texts of our culture; he already saw himself as a skeptical man, sometimes a librarian, often on the border between life and death, blind. He saw himself as the elegantly melancholic old man that he would become with time.

CHAPTER 3

The Clairvoyance of the Blindman

I was immortal. "Isidoro Acevedo," 1929[1]

FOLLOWING THE PUBLICATION of his most significant texts, and for most of the 1940s, his success in the literary world was limited. Between 1946 and 1955, he was a fervent opponent of the government of Juan Domingo Perón, and for political reasons, lost the humble library job on which he had been depending up to then. The context was not favorable to his career and he would have to wait until the middle of the 1950s for the enthronement process surrounding his figure to set in. Despite some recognition (in 1950 he was elected president of the Argentine Society of Writers, for example), it wasn't until 1955 that he would be recognized as a "Great author," in particular through his nomination to the head of the Argentine National Library by the military government that ousted Perón. Borges would ardently defend this de facto regime and his political positions would greatly influence his reception in the years to come. Only at the end of the 1960s, with the emergence of a few writers as progressive as they were innovative, highly influenced by

Borges's work (Ricardo Piglia and Juan José Saer, for example), would this situation forever change.

That is when he would begin to be called *doctor honoris causa* in national universities, when he would become a professor of English and North American Literature at the university of Buenos Aires, and would be given, in 1956, the most prestigious literary prize in Argentina (the "Premio Nacional de Literatura"). As early as the second half of the 1950s, critical works would begin to be published about him, sometimes written by well-known figures; some films based on his storylines were also made at this time.

It was also during the 1950s that he would acquire international visibility for the first time. The phenomenon began in France; Dieu La Rochelle, following a visit to Buenos Aires in 1933, had written an article on Borges the title of which is frequently quoted: "Borges is worth the journey." In the 1950s, some texts began to be translated. In 1951, Roger Callois, who spent the war years in Argentina and got to know Borges (he even had a heated discussion over the detective novel with him), founded Gallimard's collection "La Croix du Sud," with the objective of introducing great twentieth-century Latin American writers. The inaugural volume of this collection would be *Fictions*. The first English translations would be published shortly after (*Labyrinths* and *Fictions* in 1962, *Dreamtigers* in 1964, *Other Inquisitions* in 1965) broadening the recognition of Borges's work, which would soon attract the attention of writers and critics in the United States.[2]

So it was from France that the first readings of Borges by a nonspecialist of the Hispanic world would emerge, with approaches that would set political issues aside from the beginning. Maurice Blanchot dedicated a chapter, "Literary Infinity," of his *The Book to Come* to Borges in 1959. And in 1961, Borges would be awarded the Formentor Prize, tying with Samuel Beckett; the international scope of this award (it was created by a group of European and American editors; Roger Caillois was part of the jury representing Gallimard) would ensure him global notoriety from then on. In 1966, Michel Foucault would begin *The Order of Things* with a remark on a Borgesian enumeration. In the United States, Paul De Man would praise him in a 1964 article ("A Modern Master"[3]); John Updike and John Barth would do the same with "The Author as Librarian" in 1965 and "The Literature of Exhaustion" in 1967 respectively.[4] Furthermore, it is absolutely remarkable that his *Autobiographical Essay* was written (or rather dictated to Norman Thomas di Giovanni) in English and published in 1970 in the *New Yorker*, well before its translation and publication in Spanish.

These names and texts would set the tone for an assiduous reception, largely independent from readings by specialists of the Hispanic world, that continues to this day. Borges began to travel at the beginning of the 1960s (a long trip to the United States in 1961 then to Europe in 1963); he was amazed by the honors he received and enchanted by everything he "saw"—he was already blind. He who had not left Argentina since 1924 would travel the entire world until his death.

A New Skill

However, after the publication of *Other Inquisitions* and "The South," Borges would publish few original texts; the small number of books that came out at the time were various republications, including those found in the collection of his complete works created in 1953. Bioy Casares, whose personal journal contains an abundance of writing about Borges, observed that during this time, Borges was giving conferences, writing prefaces, publishing anthologies, and actively participating in political and literary life, but actually writing very little: merely a few poems and some short stories. The explanation for this change seems to be simple: in the middle of the 1950s, despite several different operations and therapeutic treatments, Borges was almost blind, due to a hereditary condition from which his father and other members of his family had also suffered. Little by little, he would cease to be able to read and write unassisted, he would require help to move about and would eventually no longer be able to recognize someone sitting right in front of him. In terms of his biography as well as of his self-representation, blindness is a major factor that constitutes the third pillar of the mythical figure of Borges. Blindness would change his relationship to creation.

First of all, the inclination toward the rewriting of his own texts would be accentuated: to a certain extent, his work could be seen as already finished, he could therefore only offer up variations on his published texts as well as on his autobiographical story (variations on this second aspect are plentiful, as we have already demonstrated). His prodigious memory would become a writing tool, and his memory would seem to become even stronger; numerous anecdotes tell of how Borges would punctuate conversations, even the most informal ones, by quoting entire poems and long passages of books in prose, or how he would give tours of the National Library, opening books and reciting certain excerpts from memory when he could no longer read.

At the time same, his liking for short forms would be confirmed; he would declare at the time having come back to poetic writing because of the ease with which he could mentally write it, which would also explain why he would prefer regular metrics over free verse from then on: "In fact, blindness made me take up the writing of poetry again. Since rough drafts were denied me, I had to fall back on memory. It is obviously easier to remember verse than prose, and to remember regular verse forms rather than free ones. Regular verse is, so to speak, portable."[5] For a period of time, poems would replace fictional prose, even as stories: "In my later poetry, a narrative thread is always to be found. As a matter of fact, I even think of plots for poems."[6] These explanations simplify the matters at hand: Borges had written a certain amount of rhyming poetry in the 1930s and 1940s, and even at the beginning of his blindness, he would continue to stay close to free verse and to produce stories in prose (most of the texts from the first part of *The Maker* [1960] date, indeed, back to the end of the 1950s).

Another significant consequence of his blindness was the development of collaborative writing. Although Borges had already developed a great literary complicity with Adolfo Bioy Casares, and they did work together, in kinship as much as for amusement (as the abounding bibliography that begins at the end of the 1930s attests), the impossibility of writing without assistance would exacerbate the desire to take on a great number of books with others, often with women who would serve as his readers and his secretaries and who would then co-sign the final product. These works are erudite, on subjects as diverse as Buddhism, English literature, American literature, medieval Germanic literatures, the animals of fantasy literature, and *Martín Fierro*. Furthermore, though a great number of young people—in particular students—spent time with him, reading or writing according to his dictation, it was above all his mother who would take on this role, occupying a central position in the continuance of her son's work. Borges would become an oral writer, but the process would require adaptation; at the end of the 1960s, he declared having found his rhythm and the technique necessary to take on a new book of short stories, *Brodie's Report* (1970).

Be that as it may, once again a life event is turned into an aesthetic choice; on several levels, not only on a political one, Borges becomes more traditional, more classical, more conservative in his exaltation of the past—an exaltation of what has already been read to the detriment of what happens on a daily basis, in other words, of what might be there to discover and to read for the first time.

A Fertile Old Age

Let what has just been said not be taken either as a moral judgement putting forth the idea that the rest of his production might be nothing but the grim repetition of that of the 1940s, or as a sign indicating that his writing was drying up, and even less as an actualization of the *topos* that inscribes disenchantment and loss of vitality in an author's old age. As with the 1938 accident, Borges incorporates this new biographical element into his style, into the way he conceives of literature, and—not surprisingly—into a renewed authorial figure. Even if his bibliography from the 1950s is thin, that decade remains an exception: two great books about this period that serve to close it out would be published shortly after: *El hacedor* (1960) and *El otro, el mismo* (1964). From that point on and up to the end of his life his literary production would increase; in addition to these two volumes, not less than eight poetry books, three stories, a voluminous collaborative work, and a great many prefaces and conferences would be published. In order to measure the production of this period in terms of length, we can refer to material data: the entire second volume of *La Pléiade* is dedicated to the period beginning in 1960, as are more than two volumes out of the four that make up the posthumous edition of his *Complete Works* published by Emecé in Argentina.

In addition to these works, we must also add interviews. He gave an immense number and they were often later compiled; in fact, their importance is proportional to his fame at the end of his life and to the obligations of his blindness. Of course, repetitions are quite frequent, but we also find some surprises; he often revisits his autobiographical story, in one way or another, and sometimes gives explanations that tend to render readings of them more complex. In any case, the volumes that compile his conversations with writers, critics, and journalists can be counted by the dozens (this transcribed and published "oral" production might have the same length as the rest of his published work); a quick search on the internet suffices to find a great many interviews recorded on the radio or filmed, including in English. One of the most surprising facts about this mass of interviews is that Borges repeats not only sentences or statements produced on other occasions (often a long time ago), he also repeats *texts* already published and the assumptions that determined his writing of them; he therefore offers a panoramic and exhaustive view of his work, all the while constantly seeking to emphasize his decisions, articulations, and effects.

"Fame, like my blindness, had been coming gradually to me," he affirms in his *Autobiographical Essay*, associating the two phenomena.[7] Yet Borges would not neglect to emphasize the paradoxical aspect of this simultaneity. To a certain extent, both would modify the primary characteristics of his image. The famous blindman, the wise blindman, is no longer exactly a son and a hero. For if the son is he who reads, who puts himself in a position to learn and to confront different texts, versions, and interpretations, the blindman is he who has read and who, therefore, knows. If the hero is he who founds, inaugurates, and transforms, the wiseman is he who contemplates constructions of the past with condescending lucidity; his gaze is retrospective, which accentuates a certain anachronistic, idealistic, and transhistorical conception of literature.

After 1955 Borges would live more than thirty years of literary life (he died in 1986), during which this posture would unfold to strongly influence his image, in terms of iconography, and his character, in terms of the type of writer he would be seen as, rendering the messianism of his youth and the ambitions of his mature age less visible. It is as a wise blindman that he would travel the world as a living emblem of the Great writer; it was he who would follow the apotheoses of his recognition earned late in life with irony and discrete satisfaction. And with some frustration, despite it all: he never got the Nobel prize, which he waited for, in vain, for years, and which, it is said, was refused him owing to some of his political views (he would often sarcastically proclaim that it was promised to him for so long that the jury in Stockholm must have thought that he had already been awarded it). And it was in this context that he would construct the last great mythical element of his biography: his own death and posterity.

The following pages will focus on a few important moments in this process.

The Gifts of a Maker

The Maker, a collection that brings together texts written between 1934 and 1960, was published in 1960. Borges specifies, in the epilogue, that they were not compiled by him but by time, which explains why some of them are "outdated," for they were written "with a different concept of literature."[8] However, he also affirms, at the same time, that none of his books are as personal as this one. It is made up of two different series, the first composed of texts in prose, the second of poems. Between the two appears "Borges and I" (the last text in prose), a kind of reflection on his writerly character, and "Poem of the Gifts" (the first poem), which is the text that most clearly exposes the paradoxes of blindness. These texts, interpretations of which are very commonly found in Borgesian exegesis, offer a sketch of the legendary features of the figure of Borges as a famous blindman.

"Borges and I" begins with duplication, reflection, and tension surrounding the writer's identity, torn between two instances in conflict, the figure of the author (Borges as a public figure) and the first person who speaks (the I).[9] The fame evoked above is integrated through this Borgesian self-representation. The differentiation announced in the title (Borges/I) is both the subject of the text and the guiding principle of its construction. Basically, it is a question of confronting the characteristics of each, similar but faintly different: on the one hand, the proper noun Borges (whom he refers to in the third person), and on the other, the deictic system I/me.

This grammatical anomaly is developed throughout the text whose incipit is a perfect example of the duplication at hand: "It's Borges, the other one, that things happen to. I walk through Buenos Aires and I pause—mechanically now, perhaps—to gaze at the arch of an entryway and its inner door; news of Borges reaches me by mail, or I see his name on a list of academics or in some biographical dictionary" (324). The author appears, at least at first, to be a character created by the "I" but who progressively gains in autonomy and eventually takes over. The likes and interests of the "I" are eventually perverted: "Borges shares those preferences, but in a vain sort of way that turns them into the accoutrements of an actor." The life of the "I" is subject to the control exerted by the other: "I live, I allow myself to live, so that Borges can spin out his literature, and that literature is my justification," without in any way entirely protecting him from death: "I am doomed—utterly and inevitably—to oblivion, and fleeting moments will be all of me that survives in that other man" (324).

This is how the consequences of the emergence of an autonomous writerly image are deployed, as are the effects of this image on the literary production process. We are therefore presented with several different "Borgeses"— the "creolist" or the avant-gardist of the 1920s, the speculative cosmopolite of the 1940s—all the while learning of the books to come: "Years ago I tried to free myself from him, and I moved on from the mythologies of the slums and outskirts of the city to games with time and infinity, but those games belong to Borges now, and I shall have to think up other things" (324).[10]

Beyond the discrepancy between the character and the biographical person, beyond any kind of reminder of the steps taken to construct the myth of Borges as a writer, the text destabilizes the unit of the subject through its strange use of verbal subjects; in doing so, the notion of an origin of any literary work is rendered ambiguous: "So my life is a point-counterpoint, a kind of fugue, and a falling away—and everything winds up being lost to me, and everything falls into oblivion, or into the hands of the other man. I am not sure which of us it is that's writing this page" (324). The effects of fame are manifested in the depersonalization of the self, absorbed as it is by the character; furthermore, this affirmation builds on Borges's quintessential theme of the author as an empty body, or one that, by writing, assumes the "link with death," to borrow Foucault's expression in "What is an author?"[11] What is presented here as a conflict would not last; in the prologue of *Brodie's Report*, Borges concludes: "advanced age has taught me to resign myself to being Borges."[12]

The second text, "Poem of the Gifts," is quite frequently cited by the writer when, in the following years, he would answer questions about the loss of his sight. In this poem, he exposes what he calls one of God's "ironies": having given him both blindness and the largest conceivable library in Argentina, the National Library. This coincidence certainly explains why he consistently dated his blindness back to 1955, the year he obtained the position as director of the institution although, on other occasions, he claimed that his loss of sight was progressive.

The poems starts off by exposing this paradox:

> No one should read self-pity or reproach
> into this statement of the majesty
> of God, who with such splendid irony
> granted me books and blindness at one touch.[13]

The tone is set: it is not a matter of complaining about his blindness, but of making something literary out of this incongruous situation by giving it meaning or higher purpose; blindness was, for him, a "gift" that corresponded to "God's" will. For the masters of this "city of books" are "sightless eyes," eyes that can read only in "libraries of dream." Consequently, the accumulation of knowledge is superfluous:

> Cultures of East and West, the entire atlas,
> encyclopedias, centuries, dynasties,
> symbols, the cosmos, and cosmogonies
> are offered from the walls, all to no purpose. (95)

The paradox quickly becomes legendary: the "infinite" number of books that he possesses suddenly become as inaccessible as the manuscripts "that perished once in Alexandria." He sees himself as Midas, who can touch nothing that surrounds him: "From hunger and from thirst (in the Greek story), / a king lies dying among gardens and fountains"; he can but wander aimlessly through "the confines / high and profound, of this blind library":

> In shadow, with a tentative stick, I try
> the hollow twilight, slow and imprecise—
> I, who had always thought of Paradise
> in form and image as a library. (95)

The paradox is not only raised to a mythical level (the Library of Alexandria, Midas, Paradise), he also introduces a parable on greed and possession; arriving in Paradise, managing to obtain everything most desired in the world, while at the same time, being prevented from taking advantage of it—quite an unusual fate.

Then the poem seeks to give meaning to this ironic situation; it is certainly not fate that "arranges all these things." Once again, repetition and identification with a figure from the past are used to justify this situation: "another man was given, on other evenings / now gone, these many books." Therefore,

> wandering through the gradual galleries
> I often feel with vague and holy dread

> I am that other dead one, who attempted
> the same uncertain steps on similar days. (95)

Here, the ultimate Borgesian theme, repetition (the actions of each man as an echo or duplication of those of another), is updated. This duplication leads us to consider the second to last stanza of "Poem of the Gifts": "Which of the two is setting down this poem— / a single sightless self, a plural I?" (97). And finally, in the last line, the sacred horror produced by the repetition subsides to leave us with a serene and melancholic image of a world loved: "this dear world losing shape, fading away/ into a pale uncertain ashy-gray / that feels like sleep, or else oblivion" (97).

Borges often contended that blindness was a blessing—a gift— and referred to this poem, as the writer could benefit from it in literary terms: the extensions of this poem in the years to come are an attempt to substantiate this idea. Here, Mallarmé's maxim— the world exists to result in a book—finds its radical confirmation. During the many years that remained before his death, Borges would often refer to blindness as one of the greatest particularities he had as a writer; a few years later, he even published a collection of poems with a title, *In Praise of Darkness* (1969), that proclaims straight away the literary positivity of his lack of sight by associating it, as he often did, with death, *his* death that he was awaiting without fear. In the poem that lends its title to the collection, "In Praise of Darkness," he comes back to heroic identifications (this time with Democritus who "plucked out his eyes in order to think"), as well as to statements about the gentleness of blindness: "This penumbra is slow and does not pain me; / it flows down a gentle slope, / resembling eternity"; at the same time, he reveals his serenity in the face of death, which gives meaning to his entire life:

> I reach my center,
> my algebra and my key,
> my mirror.
> Soon I will know who I am.[14]

The fact that he was blind constantly overtook the physical dimension to become a symbol, a paradoxical symbol of lucidity. Blindness reinforced and strengthened certain traits of the melancholic son, this time in the form of an extreme clairvoyance that counteracted a limitation and brought about, yet again, a writing agenda: "Now the world is all inside me and I see better, for I can see all the things I dream" he stated in 1962.[15] The biographical subject recedes to leave room for a writer, a Borges who would take up all the space and would turn blindness into an emblem of creation.

Being Homer

Coming back to the entire collection, which is rather eclectic, as we have said, we can advance the idea that *The Author* is, in part,—and this explains the title—made up of portraits of writers onto whom Borges projects, more or less transparently, his own image. In his autobiographical story, we go from the foundation of Buenos Aires or of Tlön to, in this case, a mere recognition of the feeling of being: the fictitious identity of the author is the main focus, at the expense of reading and writing. In one of the book's preliminary texts, Borges justifies his dedication to Leopoldo Lugones by inventing an impossible scene: Borges going, with reverence, to see Lugones in the office he occupied as director of a library in order to bring him this book. Lugones, as Borges explains it, accepted it for "Unless I am mistaken, you didn't dislike me, Lugones, and you'd have liked to like some work of mine."[16]

A true, though imaginary, reconciliation with Lugones, who died in 1938, is represented; he reconciles with the canonical author of the 1920s who had been the brunt of attacks by the young Borges. This imaginary reuniting is not far from Borges's claim to "be" a writer rather than to "do" writerly things (writing); from the start, Borges rekindles with this Great author of Argentine literature, before moving on to perusals of portraits of other authors, a series of heroic identifications with the biggest names in universal literature. This element must be considered in order to understand the insistence with which Borges would write homages to great figures of the past, writers and warriors alike.

In the first story of *The Maker*, which lends its title to the collection, we find the story of the genesis of Homer's literary vocation (Homer, as we know, is a writer invented by tradition and, according to legend, was blind).[17] The text first paints a portrait of an average person who has no awareness of time or any lucidity with regard to his condition ("He had never lingered among the pleasures of memory. Impressions, momentary and vivid, would wash over him"), his life being governed by the senses ("the smoothness of marble"; the taste of wild boar meat," honey, and wine; the sound of "a Phoenician word," the sight of a spear) and by "satisfaction and immediate difference." Then, one day, "the splendid universe" began to "draw away from him" (292); he was becoming blind. Despair would lead him to descend into his memory and conjure a memory of being insulted, a memory of transmission (his father put a bronze knife in his hands and said "Let it be known that you are a man" [293]), and of being victorious in a battle. Other memories follow, sexual ones for example, all "without bitterness, like some mere foreshadowing of the present" (293). Blindness and memorial introspection would finally lead him to understand that "love and adventure [. . .], Aries and Aphrodite" were awaiting him, along with "a rumor of glory and hexameters, a rumor of men who defend a temple that the gods will not save, a rumor of black ships that set sail in search of a beloved isle, the rumor of the *Odyssey*s and *Iliad*s that it was his fate to sing and to leave echoing in the cupped hands of human memory" (293).

Borges's identification with Homer, the first writer as far as Western culture is concerned, is unequivocal, and the value given to blindness is too—loss of sight is the trigger for writing. To write is to build out of memories and pasts; these are the elements that would lead to the emergence of a virtual life, a life shaped by a "rumor of glory and hexameters" (293) that of *The Iliad* and *The Odyssey*.

The same goes for Shakespeare, the central figure of Anglo-Saxon literature that Borges loved so much. The Englishman is also represented through the lens of subject cancellation, this time thanks to theater: masks, false identities, and changing appearances. In "Everything and Nothing," following the biography told through evocations of masks and pretenses, Shakespeare, on his deathbed, says to God, "I, who have been so many men in vain, wish to be *one*, to be myself." And out of a whirlwind, the voice of God replied "I, too, am not I; I dreamed the world as you, Shakespeare, dreamed your own work, and among the forms of my dream are you, who like me are many, yet no one."[18] If, according to a footnote in "Tlön, Uqbar, Orbis Tertius," "all men who speak a line of Shakespeare are William Shakespeare,"[19] Shakespeare, like all other men and women, and like God, is no one.

The process intensifies the reverie taking place in "Pierre Menard"; it is no longer a matter of writing a classic, but of being a great writer. For the destruction of the specificity of a foundational literary figure (Shakespeare), a father, a hero of creation, has enormous consequences: if all men and women are but a dream, Shakespeare, Homer, and even God included, anyone can be Shakespeare, Homer, or God, Borges included. Blindness, the emptying of the self, the inexistence of a stable identity, do not only give value to the other: they are above all the condition that makes it possible for the self to be seen as another, like the great writer granted recognition thanks to tradition. A double movement can be seen here. On the one hand, it is not a matter of writing (nor of rewriting like Menard), nor even of reading, but of being: being Homer, being Shakespeare (or, in other texts from the book, being Dante, being Quevedo, being Aristotle), being the authority, being the director of the National Library. And on the other hand, it is a matter of representing these model figures alongside death, skepticism, old age, and the loss of their power, which is the preamble to Borges's paradoxical process of identification. He legitimizes his own construction as an author by deconstructing what others have created.

In the book's epilogue, "J.L.B.," offers a parable that tells, quite transparently, of the way this obsession over "being" a writer works. We read, "A man sets out to draw the world. As the years go by, he peoples a space with images of provinces, kingdoms, mountains, bays, ships, islands, fishes, rooms, instruments, stars, horses, and individuals. A short time before he dies, he discovers that that patient labyrinth of lines traces the lineaments of his own face."[20] Nothing could be clearer.

The Wiseman

The Maker, as a whole, constitutes an important step; the book takes up two important phenomena of the 1950s (blindness and fame) in a kind of oxymoronic relationship: the utmost *incapacity* that blindness implies in someone who has just achieved the utmost *capacity* to circulate, give his opinion, and be seen in the literary field. Or, to cite "Poem of Gifts," the magnificent irony of God who simultaneously places him at the head of the Library and takes his sight. Borges would become the master of an entire culture's library, but only thanks to a rift, a weakness, a deficit. In 1960, his writing completes the construction of the character in integrating two significant modifications, one personal (blindness, quickly transformed into an image and a textual phenomenon), the other of a social order (national and international recognition that would crescendo up to the apotheosis of the 1980s).

A demonstration of wisdom underlies these two images: the blindman is he who has read and lived and who now, through thought, turns his gaze toward the past, with modest lucidity; he is the one who is able to leave the baroque and impetuous youth behind in order to arrive at "a rather modest and secret complexity."[21] Borges thus embodies literature in all its fullness thanks to this character, the one leaning on his cane, eyes rolling and often looking up, speaking in a composed voice broken by interruptions that give a poetic cadence to his speech (in Spanish with an accent from a completely different time period, with traces of the nineteenth century, that is, before the massive waves of immigration that would change the way Argentines speak). What's more, he punctuated his interviews and public interventions with quotes, often in other languages (English, French, German, Latin), and accumulated erudite references and ironic comments about himself. And to top it off with the ultimate sign of wisdom, he readily referred to death without it phasing the composure of his voice, and even declared that he was impatiently awaiting it, for his time on earth was up. The picture painted here corresponds quite well to an archetype of wisdom: erudition, old age, lucidity, serenity, indifference to the noises of the world. These characteristics gave him tremendous power of seduction with regard to the public: Borges became a superstar who filled halls with fascinated people.

To accompany this image, actual iconography is not lacking. During these last years, visual images of Borges often went along with his texts. For example, with the publication of the first edition of the *Complete Works* in French (*Œuvres complètes*, La Pléiade, 1993), purchasers were given a complimentary third volume made up of nothing but photos of Borges, especially those taken in mature age; the image here was meant to complete the work. Another example is that of *Atlas* (1984), a book made up of a series of notes he took during the final trips taken with María Kodama accompanied by photos. In both cases, we see Borges in a hot air balloon, Borges at Saint-Mark's square in Venice, Borges in front of Saint-Sophie's in Istanbul, Borges with a tiger—his animal symbol, Borges next to a Gallic sculpture, Borges in the supposedly labyrinthine ruins of Cnossos in Crete, Borges at the center of a spiral staircase at a hotel in Paris's Latin Quarter, Borges sitting behind a window that multiplies his reflection, Borges on Ramon Llull street in Majorca, Borges's hand on a Japanese inscription carved into stone, and, of course, the image most commonly seen, Borges in a library. Furthermore, a considerable number of caricatures from the time exaggerated his features, lending even more importance to his image. Everything was as if his face, which had become iconic, was now inseparable from his writings and, for that reason, it was also necessary to the reading of his texts.

This archetypal figure of the erudite wiseman turned Borges into the quintessential judge on literary (and other) questions; he would be asked his opinion about everything, answers to all problems were sought in his works, and subtle or barely suggested intentions would constantly be attributed to him. As for him, he would never stop preparing anthologies, planning collections of the best writers of universal literature, writing benevolent prefaces, and acting like a supreme judge on all matters of aesthetics and art. Despite the contradictory image that we have seen, and despite the paradoxical thoughts that mitigate his attitudes and value judgements, or, on the contrary, thanks to his assimilation of the distance taken by the modern critic and to his skepticism surrounding the unity and plenitude of the self, Borges, at the end of his life, would adapt and modernize the role of the author-demiurge, a concept that had begun to develop in the nineteenth century in the West and that, at the time, seemed to be no longer accepted.

A Cyclical Agony

The first edition of the *Complete Works* came out in 1974 in Buenos Aires. After his complete poetry in 1969, this was the next step toward the construction of a coherent whole: from then on, all his books would be transformed into The Book, to mention an object that was often regarded as sacred in his texts. Despite its 1,145 pages, the carefully bound volume was a tremendous success: Borges was even sold at magazine stands in Argentina. As always, he made changes to this edition, modifying for example the composition of one collection or another, and, as always, writing an introductory text and an epilogue. The introduction is simply a long dedication to his mother (who died in 1975 at the age of ninety); however, the text that he planned to place at the end of the book is quite unusual and integrates a new biographical element: posterity.

In fact, he reproduces the entry "Borges, Jorge Francisco Isidoro Luis" found in the imaginary collection *Enciclopedia Sudamericana* published in Santiago, Chile, in 2074. Some of his literary preferences and biographical facts, all well known, are enumerated in this text, which exposes, yet again, some of the aesthetic choices found in his works (such as his suspicion of the novel). With a somewhat controversial tone, he even makes his position known on popular culture as well as on literate culture (to defend the validity of the former), on the language of his time, and even on politics (he could still be identified as conservative).

It would be tempting to go further into the description and analysis of this text, which is quite strange. But let it suffice to say that it serves to foresee (and therefore to direct) the reception of his work a century ahead of time. Stendhal wagered on being read in 1935, but his projection toward the future corresponded to the *topos* of a posterity that was supposed to generate appreciation of what a genius author's contemporaries neglected to grasp. This is not what was at stake here, for Borges was at the height of his glory. At seventy-five he was, instead, beginning to worry about the future; in his situation and at his age, his concerns became literary heritage and ways to prolong an existence that would come eventually to an end. What writer will he be next? By taking place a century later, the text circumvents the inevitability of what awaits in the near future. Another figure of Borges begins to be sketched out here, a figure that completes that of the wise blindman, the last and certainly most unexpected of his avatars: Borges portrays his own death.

Two stories of the "last" Borges are useful to introduce this image. The stories develop the apparatus used in "Borges and I" by staging a meeting between two incarnations of the writer living in two different time periods: "The Other" (pre-published the same year as the *Complete Works* in Spanish, then included in *The Book of Sand*, 1975) and "August 25, 1983" (published in March 1983, which is an important detail as the story is a kind of prefiguration of what might happen in August of that year). These two tales transform the questions of death and posterity into stories.

In "The Other," we read the story of the first encounter between a Borges who finds himself in 1968 in Cambridge, Massachusetts, on the banks of the Charles, and a young Borges who is in Geneva on the banks of the Rhône at an undefined date (though we know that the writer lived there between 1914 and 1919). The old man, presented with all the traits of a famous author, is the narrator of this bizarre exchange. The relationship between them is almost like that of a father and a son in that we sense some form of self-engendering or self-filiation. But the dialogue they establish is problematic. Both subjects dominate. First with respect to literary tastes: those of the young man seem naïve to his elder, as do his political opinions and his general aesthetics ("Each of us was almost a caricature of the other"[22]); the elderly Borges thereby finds his youthful alter ego and delegitimates the choices made in these fields, which tends to reinforce the writer's later preferences.

A good amount of their exchanges then center around the explanation of their encounter, as the young man does not believe it and demands proof. The resolution of the enigma is dreamlike, as we read in the last lines of the story: it is suggested that the younger Borges has in fact dreamt up the encounter. The older Borges is therefore the product of his own dream—and not of God's dream as Shakespeare was in "Everything and Nothing"—a creation dreamt up in youth. Consequently, Borges, the great Borges of old age, *doctor honoris causa* at universities across the world, is but the product of his desire, a longstanding desire, the desire of a pre-adolescent wandering along the banks of the Rhône River during the First World War.

After its prepublication in the newspaper *La Nación*, the second story, "August 25, 1983," would be integrated in Borges's unfinished last book, *Shakespeare's Memory*. It is a variation on the previous story: two Borgeses of different ages meet, have a discussion, and do not agree on anything. They are both living out the same day, an August twenty-fifth, but the years vary; this time the narrator is the younger one who lives in 1960, while his alter ego is in 1983. The title refers to the date at which the older of the two decided to commit suicide (the story is a fictionalization of Borges's 1934 suicide attempt) and their exchange lasts until the older one dies. What this story represents is therefore impossible, that is, the story of his own agony and death; the younger one even notes the writer's last words ("And it won't be tomorrow, either—it will be many years from now"[23]). Once again, the plot provides us with an explanation for the encounter from the world of dreams; the older one, in referring to what is happening to him, begins by saying: "It is, I am sure, my last dream."[24] Indeed, when the narrator leaves the room, after the death of the other Borges, he does not regain reality, but instead finds other dreams awaiting. The scene was in fact Borges's last dream.

This story's apparatus implies, in a way, a negation of death: he who dies is not exactly me, but the other. In 1983, Borges finds his 1960 double, and this death is called to repeat itself, inevitably, every twenty-three years. With these conditions, upon his own death, he can still say, "you still have many years." In fact, this story builds on the possibility that was implied in "The Other": old age, blindness, death, in an endless cycle, will begin again in a kind of delicate eternity. A young man, when he grows up, will find another young man along the banks of a river, and when the grown man arrives at the last second of his life, he will have another younger man by his side, who will then slowly grow old. Both at the summit of his glory as a writer and in agony, a scene of transmission is played out between the father-self and the son-self, from the elderly self to the mature self. Old age is a time for discovering death, but this discovery and what is learned from it go on indefinitely. The change in perspective is also significant; in "The Other," the narrator is an experienced writer who arrives at truth but who turns out to be but a young man's dream; in "August 25, 1983," the young narrator is the product of the desire of the old man on his deathbed. Both have many years of life and writing ahead. Death, the ultimate unique experience, becomes malleable and multiple.

We could extend this analysis in turning to "Shakespeare's Memory," which lends its title to a posthumous collection. We again find the question of transmission, the supernational transmission of the Bard's memory, accomplished through a mere oral pact, to the story's protagonist (a German specialist of Shakespeare living at the beginning of the twentieth century). The narrator, who starts off by affirming that his "fate has been Shakespeare,"[25] then carries a double memory for several years: his own and that of another. He remains who he always was but he also, to a certain extent, becomes Shakespeare. He lives out his everyday life all the while experiencing a life that is "a great deal more extraordinary than Shakespeare's"[26]). But when this other memory begins to threaten his own, he decides to pass it on to a stranger.

This fable in turn dramatizes the act of transmission: it is no longer a matter here of writing what another already wrote, nor even of becoming another, but rather of ensuring the perpetuation of generations and identities, a portion of the "I" that would otherwise be fated to disappear. The story also fits into an auto-filiation, superposing the posterity of the English writer on that of the Argentine, which could already be foreseen: in passing on the memory of another, one attempts also to translate one's own. According to this fable, there is something that does live on, survive, and that is inherited beyond death; Borges as Shakespeare and Shakespeare as Borges may continue to exist.

The Immortal Dead Man

To conclude this somewhat imaginary biography, we can now question the ways these narratives are integrated into the texts on the writer's old age. The public figure of Borges at eighty years old prevents us, to a certain extent, from accurately evaluating his lifework. However, despite his omnipresence in prefaces, in the media, in homages, academic circles, and institutions, creation has not ceased. As we have already suggested, Borges's old age was just as fertile as his youth, at least if we take into account the mass of texts published, which contradicts, in a way, the imminence of the end and the loss of life.

The number of texts and his activity in the publishing world did not inspire much recognition on the part of specialized critics: Borges's being seen near the Chilean and Argentine dictatorships of the time (he was decorated by Pinochet in 1974, a year after the death of Allende; he lunched with Videla shortly after the coup d'état of 1976 in Argentina) could explain the indifference or even hostility toward what he was writing at the time. The most well-known sentence of all his late books, from the preface of "The Iron Coin," is also the most unworthy and the least forgivable that he would ever write. We read, "I am well aware that I am unworthy of uttering opinions on political matters, but perhaps I might be forgiven for doing so by adding that I have doubts about democracy, that curious abuse of statistics. Buenos Aires, July 27, 1976."[27] The coup d'état had just taken place in Argentina, and terror reigned over the country's intellectuals and progressives. Other statements and facts lead us in the same direction; later, he would admit his miscalculation with regard to his political opinions. This remains, nonetheless, the writer's darkest side. After several years of tension generated by this element of his character, posterity would rightly choose to forget his diversions, his political blindness.

But whatever the reason for the indifference on the part of critics toward his late productions, it would be false to say, as has been done, that he was reduced to a mere repetition. In his final books, Borges weaves and unweaves his blindness, his old age, and his death with his previous works, his personal past, and universal culture in an intentional effort to transform what was about to happen to him into fiction. This is the literary work of mature age, a task that Borges seems to complete with serenity and no doubt with enthusiasm. His late texts explore death, representing it through different situations and with different, sometimes opposing, values; rather than being a constant, the subject introduces proliferation. For example, when he evokes a friend from his youth, Abramowicz, he imagines a kind of immortality, "the notorious fact that no one can die,"[28] although "everyone runs the risk / of being the first immortal."[29] Elsewhere he evokes the inevitability of death:

> Jesus' pain will afford no pardon
> Nor Socrates' suffering, nor the inviolate
> Golden Siddhartha, who within the twilit
> Final hour of evening, in a garden
> Accepted death.[30]

However, "better to think of others / when the hour is near."[31] We find attempts to write about his own death in his writings on the deaths of others; the death of his grandmother in Geneva,[32] that of Xul Solar,[33] that of Francisco Luis Bernárdez in the poem "Epilogue" ("I say that you have died. I too have died"[34]) and, as a result, a representation of the afterlife:

> What errant labyrinth, what blinding flash
> Of splendor and glory shall become my fate
> When the end of this adventure presents me with
> The curious experience of death?[35]

We also find stories about this moment ("La prueba" in *The Limit*), and even the expression of his impatience with regard to it. We read,

"I am doomed [. . .] to want to sink myself into death and to not be able to do so, to be and to continue to be," and even,

> I await one thing not yet tasted
> a gift, gold from the shadows
> this virgin
> death.[36]

Death is a fertile subject; it generates contrasted and paradoxical writing in which the figures of authority for Borges are summoned one after the other: "Macedonio Fernández, so fearful of death, explained to us that dying is the most trivial thing that can befall us."[37] These texts seek to be read like a self-written epilogue or epitaph: "I am that other one who saw the desert / and in his eternity goes on watching it. / I am a mirror, an echo. The epitaph."[38]

In all these texts, the temporal labyrinth, which in some of Borges's other writings so deeply disturbed the past, opens, this time, onto the future; on these occasions, the temporal instability concerns what is to come. "I am no one," Borges often wrote, a paradox that laid out another: the "I am dead" of the end of his life. The position taken in both statements is conflictual and confounding given the incompatible terms he chooses to express himself in an attempt to elude the imperatives of reason and of human life in general. What is at stake resembles the conception of belief according to psychoanalysis: "I know well, but all the same."[39] Literature is this "all the same" that incessantly casts doubt on what is nonetheless imminent:

> The Arabs say no-one can ever
> read right through the Book of the Nights.
> The Nights are Time, which never sleeps.
> Keep reading as the day declines and
> Scheherazade will tell you your own story.[40]

Borges, in drafting the story of the end of his life, places himself between two deaths, after the death of the great writers, of his characters, of his parents, and even after his own death. He places himself between a symbolic, narrated, textual death, and his actual death; indeed, he creates a prophetic space that can be seen as a loss, as well as an event in the past, but not as an inevitable border toward which we are heading. In this way, the unknown is incorporated into the known and the unforeseeable into the pages already written. In these conditions, the few bits of a storyline about the actual agony that Borges experienced take on an interesting meaning. Jean-Pierre Bernès explains that Borges never complained but did express concern about knowing in which language he would die. It is also said that during his final days, he requested, on several occasions, to be read the passage on the death of Alonso Quijano, the man who thought he was Quixote in Cervantes's novel. These are his final attempts to die in literature.

The terminal image of Borges is therefore that of an immortal dead man. It would continue to function beyond that fatal day in 1986 (June 14), the same year that the author's first posthumous book, a compilation of articles written for the journal *El Hogar* in the 1930s, would be published. This would be but the first in a long series. On the eve of the year 2000, a number of works were published: three volumes of essays from his youth that Borges wanted to eliminate from his bibliography; three volumes assembling his scattered collaborations (with the significant title *Textos recobrados* [Borges recovered]); the texts published in the journal *Sur*; and books of prefaces as well as compilations of conferences and correspondence, transcriptions of courses given, countless collections of interviews, and so on. For a long time, in the circles of specialists of Argentine literature, we continued to speak of, to comment on, and to study "Borges's latest book," even though the writer had been dead for a long time.

The fervor of editors was only part of Borges's definitive transformation into a monument, a process that reached its peak in 1999 with the centennial of his birth: coins with the author's face were made in Argentina, and Serrano Street in Palermo, where his childhood home was, was renamed Jorge Luis Borges Street (rendering unreadable, it's worth noting in passing, the famous line in which he plays on the name of the street and on the way it sounds). At the same time, incessant scandals and conflicts—often quite pathetic—surrounding his legacy, his memory, and the "ownership" of Borges took place. All of this is of course understood from the perspective of the functioning of a "literary field," of the institutionalization of authors, of the sacralization of their figures, and even of a certain cultural nationalism; it would not be outrageous, however, to consider that all of this was a late effect engendered by the figure of Borges himself, an effect of this final figure that has been incessantly interpreted and reinterpreted since his death.

In "The Immortal," a story included in *The Aleph*, the protagonist manages to become immortal, then, after several centuries of wandering the earth, finds a way to return to being mortal, thus renouncing eternal life. In the last sentence of the story, the narrator states, "I have been Homer; soon, like Ulysses, I shall be Nobody; soon, I shall be all men—I shall be dead."[41] Herein we can read a prefiguration of what would end up happening about forty years after this story was written: Borges dies having been immortal; he dies immortal.

PART II
A Pensive Sentiment
Materials

I've fixed my feelings into durable words
When they could have been spent on tenderness.

"Almost a Last Judgment," 1925[1]

ITALO CALVINO ASSERTED that Borges had perfected a modality of fiction, a "Borgesian fiction" that he considered to be the latest novelty to take place in terms of literary genres. This novelty consisted in a specific kind of erudition, guided by imaginary books and potential literature.[2] Michel Lafon thought the biographical pattern played a similar role in the definition of this personal narrative form.[3] To be complete without being exhaustive, I will add two additional characteristics that distinguish the functioning as well as the semantic significance of Borges's texts: first, the dynamic that connects writing composed of clues (borrowed from police novels) to possible readings and interpretations, and second, the variations in the representation of time and therefore the links that fiction creates with history, be it literary or social.

What follows will offer a few transversal commentaries on these aspects of the Borgesian story (biography, incendiary writing, erudition, temporalities), the "story" being understood in its largest definition: short stories, essays, and poems (or at least certain poems) included. The story is, fiction is, for Borges, a way of being in the world and not only a literary form. Just as the figure of the author can be closely linked to aesthetic and semantic tendencies appearing in the works, these modalities of the story imply a conception of literature, a vision of the world, a metaphysics of the subject and of meaning.

CHAPTER 4

Impelled by His Germanic Blood

Biography and the Meaning of the Story

The truth is that his life is more interesting than his books.
"Biography of Oscar Wilde," 1938[1]

THE FIRST SENTENCES of the story "The South" paint the portrait of its protagonist, an Argentine librarian, Juan Dahlmann, grandson of a German evangelical pastor and of a *criollo* member of the military who fought in the Argentine civil wars of the nineteenth century; a small number of other personal traits are soon added to this defining biographical fact, that is, the dual nature of his national origins. Then something happens: after a serious accident, the fate of Juan Dahlmann becomes terminal and the story that tells it turns fantastic: we don't know whether he dies at the hospital—the insignificant death of a librarian, in tune with the trajectory his evangelical grandfather—or whether he dies, after a dangerous trip to a legendary pampa, in a duel with knives—an epic death like that of his military grandfather. This introduction to the character and the pages that follow represent a quite literal transposition of the writer's 1938 accident that we've already commented on, as well as of other aspects of Borges's biography.

This example allows us to introduce a first element characteristic of Borges's practice of the story: the usage of the biographical pattern as a model for narration, which engages a certain conception of narrational causality. By "biographical pattern" I mean the reduction of one of the most widespread forms of the story, the story of an individual's life, to a few basic points: origins, influences, education, major events, and the conditions of death. A form that activates the collective belief that life is one, that it is oriented, and that it has meaning.[2] If, as has already been suggested, Borges turns the question of the meaning of the universe into a catalyst for writing, a similar trend is observed with respect to the history of humankind. The biography presupposes a logical connection between the events that make it up, a causality associated with the importance of origins, first experiences, and transformative moments, and thus includes the idea of determination. The biography is a narrative structure (chronological order, emphasis on major stages or events), as well as a way of attributing meaning to the whole.

Let's have a closer look. After introducing the two grandfathers of the protagonist of "The South" (the German who landed in Buenos Aires in 1871 and had the same name as his grandson Johannes, and the Argentine Francisco Flores, who died fighting the Indians), the narrator provides an enigmatic commentary on his origins: "In the contrary pulls from his two lineages, Juan Dahlmann (perhaps impelled by his Germanic blood) chose that of his romantic ancestor, or that of a romantic death," that is, Francisco Flores. This decision is explained by the fact that the character has developed a "slightly willful but never ostentatious 'Argentinization,'" apparent in the preservation of relics (a portrait, a sword) and of certain tastes (tangos, reciting Martín Fierro).[3] This statement is essential for it becomes meaningful in retrospect, at the end of the story, when the reader suspects that Dahlmann, just as he preferred his Argentine lineage, has then chosen his death. His double origin prepares the reader for the double climax of the story: his death at the hospital and his death in a duel with knives.

Beyond the foreshadowing of the explanation of the climax that the portrait of Dahlmann introduces, this sentence is highly paradoxical: according to the hypothesis put forth, the grandson of a German pastor would prefer his heroic filiation, the noble lineage in line with Argentine nationalism, because of a romantic spirit that might be specific to the German people and therefore because of the intervention of his foreign origins. The epic Argentinity acquired is "impelled by his Germanic blood."

It is surprising to see this nationalist and familial (the German grandfather, the Germanic spirit) or even genetic (blood) determinism appear as an explanation for Dahlmann's identification, since Borges's work frequently renders the unicity of the subject relative by reiterating that each man is every man or that being is but a simulacrum. If we take into account the values and general functions of origins, it is entirely unique to conclude that German blood leads to choosing Argentine filiation. The authority of inheritance, according to the sacred principles of our myths surrounding origins, is absolute; nonetheless, here it incites Juan Dahlmann to choose the other origin, betraying himself in a way. He feels "deeply Argentine," yet it appears as if German blood were the reason for this identitarian sentiment.

The paradox (praise for the emblems of Argentine nationalism due to European influence) contains another, more ideological, one within, which Borges points out in "The Argentine Writer and Tradition," an essay included in the 1957 republishing of *Discussion*. While discussing the tendency of nationalist writers to introduce elements "typical" of a supposed Argentinity, he writes, "the Argentine cult of local color is a recent European cult that nationalists should reject as a foreign import."[4] This assessment in fact weakens the bonds of nationalism, for the concept, as Borges sees it, owes something to an ideology that is foreign and that should, in fact, be rejected for the sake of national identity.

In any case, it is easy to recognize a recurrent tension between national origins and familial determinism in the example of "The South," each of the forces acting in ways that are contrary to their basic characteristics. This opposition does not however imply the cancellation of their influence: the text exposes both the power of origins—Germanic blood is the reason for Dahlmann's behavior—and their negation, emptying, and overcoming. While Germanic blood explains the Argentinity of the character, origins are a choice and not a serious constraint. All of this points to the consistency of a dominant *topos* in Borges: the representation and development of oppositions and dichotomies, a strategy that allows him to take advantage, in terms of narration, of the semantic division produced. According to Ricard Piglia, "Borges never excludes opposites; he keeps them in the foreground and integrates them as elements inherent to his writing,"[5] which is why it can be said that the rhetorical figure of the oxymoron, if we broaden its definition, corresponds quite well to this type of conflictual exposure of meaning.

Statistics and Fate

The portrait of Juan Dahlmann is a late version of a dominant narrative model, the more or less imaginary biographical story, in Borges's texts from the 1930s, the period of progressive movement toward fiction in prose. *Evaristo Carriego* (1930) and *A Universal History of Iniquity* (1935) are the main landmarks, but we must also mention the numerous (approximately fifty) "Brief Biographies" published in the journal *El Hogar* and reproduced again in *Textos cautivos* (1936–1939). Biography, as a genre, or rather the biographical note as it appears in encyclopedias and dictionaries of authors, appears as a starting point for his fictions in the making. These notes turn the encyclopedia into narration, adventure, destiny—and even, lastly, into a form of biased autobiography; only once they have been transposed into the realm of the imaginary (invented writers, made up lives) would they become short stories.

We can therefore conclude that fiction in Borges's work emerges, in this instance, from the distortion of biographical summaries (which he called "statistical data"[6]); the unsubstantiated book review is also a component of this same trend. In any case, it can be said that all this material (the biography of Carriego, the "infamous" biographies, the "brief" biographies of writers) functions as a space for experimentation, through the accumulation of quotes, questions, and ideas that are then recycled, through the clarification of rhetorical and argumentative strategies, through the destabilization of the notion of value, and ultimately, through the unique forms of entry into literary history.[7]

Evaristo Carriego, although it appears to be a biography, is highly marked by a series of affirmations that expose Borges's disbelief in this kind of historical narrative. The second chapter, which is where the poet's life begins to be narrated, carries the unique title "A Life of Evaristo Carriego"; the use of the indefinite article "a" insinuates that other lives and other stories could have been written. This second chapter opens with a dubious speculation that increases the distance taken by the author with regard to the practice of biographical writing: "That one person should wish to arouse in another memories relating only to a third person is an obvious paradox. To pursue this paradox freely is the harmless intention of all biography."[8] Borges therefore positions himself above "frivolity" and "innocence," not to mention above the naivety of a biographical story. This type of story is presented as arbitrary and even paradoxical; "the events of his life, while infinite and incalculable" seem to be "easily recorded" (54), but are insufficient. "I believe that a chronological account is inappropriate to Carriego; far better seek his eternity, his patterns. Only a timeless description, lingering with love, can bring him back to us" (55). In neglecting chronology, Borges opts for the construction of a writerly image, which, in his opinion, is a sure sign of efficiency; he prefers a Platonian image to an uncertain destiny.

In a 1950 text, added to the book in a later edition, Borges puts forth another idea about the biographical form: "I have always suspected that any life, no matter how full or complex it may be, is made up essentially of a single moment—the moment in which a man finds out, once and for all, who he is."[9] In fact, this sentence is a variant, a re-writing, of another sentence—the process is frequent—from a story included in *The Aleph*, "A Biography of Tadeo Isidoro Cruz (1829–1874)": "Any life, no matter how long and complicated it may be, actually consists of a single moment—the moment when a man knows forever more who he is."¹⁰ Faced with a life, the facts of which are "infinite and incalculable" according to the first quote, and that is "full and complex," "long and complicated," according to the subsequent ones, Borges first responds with a transhistorical image and then with a focus on meaning and performance through the episode mentioned that, in a single stroke, gives an identity to a man and meaning to his existence. Yet, when he exposes the different problems surrounding the story of any existence, Borges not only takes a stance in favor of an "essence" of human life; he also reflects on the story in general, on its functioning, its effects, and its consistent explanations. In the first example, the response is a kind of poetic portrait (the "timeless description" of Carriego), and in the second, a brief narration centered around a punctual and disconnected effect. Consequently, the result is not a novel but a short story. In that respect, the biography, more than the story of a destiny, is a presentation of the circumstances that prepare and allow for a kind of revelation or at least some sort of eruption: "something" happens and transforms what we have come to know up to then, its enigmatic nature interfering with meaning. In Borges's biographies, this "something" that erupts is often the literary vocation and the writerly identity.

For this reason, since life is reduced to an enlightening event, his biographies function like teleological stories, taking on a formalist perspective or even becoming parodies. The most well-known example is "Conjectural Poem" (1943) in which a historical figure, Laprida, awaits his imminent death and thinks to himself:

> At last I have discovered
> the long-hidden secret of my life,
> the destiny of Francisco de Laprida,
> the missing letter, the key, the perfect form
> known only to God from the beginning.¹¹

Iniquities

The collection *A Universal History of Iniquity* is made up of one of Borges's stories ("Man on Pink Corner") and seven brief biographies of more or less historical figures presented as unique cases of the "iniquity" announced in the title: an English imposter, a Chinese female pirate, a New York crook, a false prophet from Turkmenistan, etc. These texts have an obvious connection to Marcel Schwob (just as much as to Samuel Johnson) is clear, despite Borges's repeated denial ("I did not want to repeat what Marcel Schwob had done in his *Imaginary Lives*," he wrote in his *Autobiographical Essay*[12]), though elsewhere and much later, he would admit to the influence; moreover, he had published some of the Frenchman's "lives" in the same journal as his own biographies.

In addition to the these "infamous" portraits Borges paints, we find statements borrowed from the preface of Schwob's book when Borges opposes his fragmentary, imaginary lives to the naturalist novel or the work of the historian, as well as statements that confirm the unstable and multiple nature of the biographical story: "perfection for the biographer would mean infinitely differentiating the thinking of two philosophers who had invented a metaphysics that was more or less the same."[13] In many of Borges's essays and stories, we find a similar but inversed version of this stance, as in "Theme of the Traitor and the Hero," a story in which the biography of Kilpatrick treats him as either a hero or a traitor, depending on which life events are chosen. The same possibility is mentioned in an essay included in *Other Inquisitions*, "On William Beckford's *Vathek*":

> So complex is reality, and so fragmentary and simplified is history, that an omniscient observer could write an indefinite, almost infinite, number of biographies of a man, each emphasizing different facts; we would have to read many of them before we realized that they referred to the same protagonist; an extreme case could be a biography of Michelangelo that would make no mention of the works of Michelangelo.[14]

This proliferation and the effects of his selection would be brought to bear in the writing of Borges's great stories.

As much in Schwob as in Borges, the biographical genre is reworked on the basis of a series of infractions: generic hybridization, metadiscursivity, open or hypothetical conclusions, specularity, and narrative ellipses.[15] Both authors can therefore be inscribed in what we call the modern paradigm of biography, that is, a biographical form that is aware of the limitations of the genre and that tends to include the gesture of representation rather than attempt to tell the complete and seamless life story of someone;[16] they disturb this type of story by exhibiting an indirect or diagonal truth and interfere with hierarchies (Schwob mixes the lives of "nobles" and those of the "infamous," while Borges integrates iniquity into a kind of personal pantheon); and finally, they question consistent causality. Let us also add that *A Universal History of Iniquity* turns its back on psychology and on the detailed story of a becoming in favor of quick enumeration, schematic statements, and summaries of events; as such, the stories can be considered more typologies of characters, highly affiliated with paraliterature, that is, with adventure stories, police novels, soap operas, and even Hollywood films.

The practice of biography therefore allows for the recovery and dismantling of the fundamentals of any story insofar as the mechanism of cause and effect is exposed, made fun of, or exacerbated. The best example of this aspect that structures the traditional novel and is parodied in this way can be found in the first of the iniquitous stories, "The Cruel Redeemer Lazarus Morell." At the beginning of the text, causality is expanded to an absurd and humorous extent; under the subtitle "The Remote Cause," we find a series of heterogeneous effects of the 1517 intervention of Bartolomé de Las Casas on the side of the "Indians," which led to the arrival of African slaves in the Americas. The multitude of effects include, as the narrator explains, blues music, the success in Paris of Figari (a Uruguayan painter who depicted the festivities of black communities in Montevideo), the "mythological stature of Abraham Lincoln," the half-million dead of the War of Secession, the 3.3 billion dollars spent on military pensions," and so on. A myriad of consequences are enumerated (including "the gracefulness of certain elegant young ladies") until we arrive in the end at "the evil and magnificent existence of the cruel redeemer Lazarus Morell," a hustler who traffics slaves at the beginning of the nineteenth century in the southern United States.

The short sections that follow this introduction express, with exaggeration, the consistent protocols of the traditional fictional model: after this distant "cause," we move onto the place ("The Place," with a description that hints at the plot to come), the characters ("The Men," that is to say the social milieu and the recent history that delimits the action to come), the protagonist ("The Man," a physical description and a description of the morals of Lazarus Morell), the stakes ("the Method," in other words the swindling actions typical of Lazarus, which explain the core of the plot), etc. Then, after an extremely laconic story, despite all these preliminary steps, we are projected into the conclusion, which does not emerge as the fruit of a development or as a final result, but as a sudden break in the text. Indeed, the last section carries the explicit title, "The Interruption"; the story does not finish with a scene that might correspond to the information offered or that might satisfy the expectations generated by the story, but rather by an anodyne death at a hospital: "it pains me to admit that the history of the Mississippi did not seize upon those rich opportunities. Nor, contrary to all poetic justice (and poetic symmetry), did the river of his crimes become his tomb. On the 2nd of January 1835, Lazarus Morell died of pulmonary congestion in the hospital at Natchez."[17] This outcome completes the destabilization of the plot. The story is disappointing; the key element of the biography, a conclusion capable of giving meaning to what precedes, capable of turning a life into a vocation or destiny, is absent. The rupture seems to be warranted by the historical "truth" of the conclusion, as we have here a biography of a man who actually existed: the fictional narrative, which manages to take advantage of biographical elements and stretch them out throughout the narrative, is therefore superior to the reality, which imposes a sudden resolution without much interest. Beyond the specific narrative choices (that seem here to be the opposite of those made in *Evaristo Carriego*), the practice of biography writing leads to the deployment of the story's potential, the story, in this case, parodying the fortress surrounding genre and meaning that is the novel of the Western world.

In the context of a clear obsession over filiation, nationality, significant experiences, and, in general, origins, Borges takes up and recycles, here and elsewhere, the topics of determinism: blood in terms of national or racial belonging, inheritance from parents or more distant lineages, the relationship between life and writing, the coordinates of intellectual training, the ordeals of childhood and youth viewed as the roots of a personal or artistic destiny. In doing so, his biographies never cease to respond to certain questions surrounding the literary practice: how to understand what we read, how to evaluate it, and above all, how to explain it while taking into account the life that is behind it, the emergence of the work.

The reuse of these questions and answers that often fall back on stereotypes and literary myths is paradoxical. For it is not a matter of finding answers to these questions, but of multiplying the answers, as a means to both update the absorbing and fundamental question and render its answer—necessarily simplistic and banal—insufficient. Nowhere here is there an attachment to any kind of principle that might explain the relationship between the life and the work, between origins and outcomes; we find instead a confrontation of opposing values and an ironic detachment, or perhaps disbelief. Without choosing between adhesion, obsession, and deconstruction, Borges takes up the traditional narrative patterns of biography and galvanizes them; biography is now understood as a story that is fabled without being false in the sense that rather than reaffirming certainties, it deploys the mysteries inherent to creation.

The Forms of a Life

Borges's conception of the biographical genre, as we have just seen with respect to the texts of the 1930s, would make their mark on the narrative model of a great number of stories to come, in particular those found in *Fictions*. In this collection, we find other "lives" parallel or similar to those of Dahlmann in "The South." For example, "The Circular Ruins," a fable with mythical tones, tells the story of how a magician, in an unspecified country of the Middle East at an unspecified time, takes on the superhuman task of conceiving of a man through dream and then inserting him into reality. The task of engendering a new life without sexuality is accompanied by the symbolic presence of a river, an archetypal image of linear time. The development of the plot follows the steps of this "birth into the world" of an imaginary being (attempts, failures, mediation of divine power and finally success); as the plot comes to an end, the magician discovers that he, who believed himself to be the subject and the master of the creative dream, is but the dream of another.

The story offers up an allegory of creation in that it dramatizes the acts required to obtain realistic representation, the latter emerging from dreams but destined to become a form of reality. Man, conceived of in this way, is an actor in the world, but he is only the result of the oneiric, immaterial activity of another man. In any case, in terms of origins, the result implies maximal determinism: man is but the fruit of a desire that precedes him and that dictates each moment of his existence.

"Funes, His Memory" presents a variant of this determinism of origins. The protagonist, Ireneo Funes, a young simpleminded man living in the Uruguayan pampa of the nineteenth century, acquires a supernatural gift following an accident: an infallible memory. Thanks to this gift, he can, for example, learn Latin by reading through the dictionary and recite, without hesitation, every text he consults. He also perceives reality with an extraordinary acuity, retaining the slightest details of everything he sees or hears. Yet, Ireneo is the son of a village laundry woman and a "questionable" man (perhaps an English doctor, perhaps an animal trainer, or a guide from the area); his filiation, bastard and imprecise, is that which is often attributed to *gauchos*. Which of these conditions are determined by which of these multiple origins? In other words, and following the example from "The South," are his exceptional gifts linked to his English origins or to the pampa? However, in his case, it is not ambiguous bloodlines (like Dahlmann's) that decide his fate but an accident (like for Dahlmann). After he falls off a horse, the course of his life is transformed; he becomes "a maverick and vernacular Zarathustra" according to the laudatory judgement brought about him at the beginning of the story.[18] His place of birth, nationality, and family origins are the complete opposite of the extraordinary capacities that he acquires, in particular his knowledge of Latin and of the life of illustrious men of ancient Rome. The conditioning has multiple sources this time and renders an unforeseeable outcome.

In "The Circular Ruins," just as in "The South," origin conditions destiny. In "Funes, His Memory," destiny seems, on the contrary, to complicate inherited determinism. This "backward" variation of the predictable is at the heart of the plot of another story, "The Story of the Warrior and the Captive" (in *The Aleph*), in which two symmetrical stories are opposed. First, a barbaric warrior in late antiquity forgets which tribe he belongs to, forgets "the dense forests of the wild boar" of his native lands, his beliefs, his past, and even his own people, in order to defend a Roman village that fascinated him, Ravenna, a radiant city with cypresses and marble. Then, the second story is that of an Englishwoman from Yorkshire taken captive by Indians in the nineteenth-century Argentine pampa who, after fifteen years of living among the tribe, ends up forgetting English and her European past. She adopts native values and ways of life, preferring a "savage and uncouth life" of "raids," "plunder," "battle," "polygamy," "stench," and "magic."[19] The biographies are similar, even if the shift taking place is from "barbary" to "civilization" in one, and from "civilization" to "barbary" in the other; the most striking similarity lies in the powerful negation of original determinism found in these two characters.

In this respect, Dahlmann's double filiation, mentioned at the beginning of this chapter, can be integrated into a consistent series, despite the diversity of the various stories and the contrasts they present. In one version, determination is absolute and even frightening; in another, it is sought out and desired; in one case, it is directly contradicted, and in the other, it is carried out despite apparent contradictions. This operation is coherently crystallized in certain narrative patterns imagined by Herbert Quain, a fictional writer whose biography is told and work described in "A Survey of the Works of Herbert Quain." One of his novels is comprised of a proliferation of retrospective variations. It starts with a given situation, an ambiguous conversation taking place on the platform of a train station. The chapters that follow then tell of the events that preceded this situation, but these events are not unique. Many series of divergent facts are put forward; each series is, in turn, supposed to explain the conversation recounted at the beginning, but each one does so by telling of different events. The causal chain that we can elaborate leading up to a mundane event is manifold; consequently, in this imaginary novel, nine separate novels, or at least nine separate stories, all end with the same scene (this type of apparatus circulates in the work of Italo Calvino; see his novel *If on a Winter's Night a Traveler*).

This multiplicity, we can imagine, is both a game of logic and a parodic formalization of the biographical pattern. There is, it appears, only ever one concrete reality: the work of an author. The story of the author's life, according to Borges, is the fruit of arbitrary choices made among the multiple chains of events that might or might not explain the outcome, namely the writing of the work we are reading. In another story, "The Garden of Forking Paths" (*Fictions*), a similar construction is imagined: one that presumes that every situation, every cause, leads not only to one consequence or effect, excluding all the others, but to endless forking: each fact sets off an infinite number of independent stories, located along different timelines.

Let us take stock of what we've seen so far. Despite its encyclopedic roots, the writing process reveals the arbitrary elements inherent in the story, the selection of elements that govern its logical progression, and the misleading pretension to offer answers to a question that in fact is not one. Borges, as he himself wrote with regard to the ancient Greeks and their sophisms, might have been playing into "perplexity and mystery."[20] Be that as it may, the biographical story appears as a malleable formal apparatus offering a model of causality that is either respected, parodied, or transgressed; in other words, it is an explicative dynamic that is constantly exhibited, questioned, and dramatized. If "every act crowns an infinite series of causes and causes an infinite series of effects"[21] and if every biographical story mandates the choice of certain facts among thousands, narrating a life means confronting the passage from an abundant proliferation to an intelligible story, therefore to an aporia, intelligibility being furthermore obtained by way of fiction, which renders it arbitrary though efficient. In this way, fiction reduces multiplicity and exposes a limited number of events that are supposed to explain a trajectory in either a harmonious or surprising way.

Borges discusses the inner workings of this causality in the 1930s essay "Narrative Art and Magic." We read that, as opposed to the natural process (that of reality), which is the "incessant result of endless, uncontrollable causes and effects," the process of the novel is "magic," "lucid," and "determined"; "detail is prophecy."[22] In the real world, endless proliferation also dominates: the world cannot be grasped through a limited process like a story; the framework of the story imposes architectural limits on events in order to provide at least a semblance of coherence. In this way, the novel and the short story provide an explanation of events by limiting the horizon of possibilities; the causes are, in one way or another, governed by magic.

Here, the use of the word "magic" might suggest a supernatural dimension, though what is at hand is, yet again, exacerbated determinism. "Magic is the crown or the nightmare of the law of cause and effect, not its contradiction." Faced with a chaotic world, the novel "should be a rigorous scheme of attentions, echoes, and affinities. Every episode in a careful narrative is a premonition."[23] In this respect, biography can be considered a laboratory for writing, as it allows us to take apart the patterns of causality in any story and to suggest unimaginable associations and contradictory filiations, that is, when it's not implanting parodies of its own methods.

CHAPTER 5

The Universe, *Whodunit?*
Reading and the Detective Novel

To write a book that keeps a moving angle of shadows; that corresponds in some way to the past as well as to the secret future; that no analysis can exhaust.

"De la alta ambición en el arte" [Of the high ambition of art], 1945[1]

LET US RETURN for a moment to "Pierre Menard." The story presents a wide range of misunderstandings, generational adjustments, and uncertain chronologies: who is the father, who is the son, who is the master, who is the disciple, who arrives first, who arrives later, who has influence over whom, who is who since all men are the same man and literature is a unique ensemble? In the end, who wrote *Don Quixote*?

To these questions can be added the enigma presented in a story that, like practically any other page in Borges, accumulates distorted allusions and statements, that is to say, the mechanisms made popular by detective novels. The description of Menard is conducted through so many hints and allusions that we can say it functions almost like a guessing game, the answer to which might complete the text: who "is hiding" behind Menard? Who *is* he? The diligent interpretation of these hints has led Borgesian criticism to offer diverging answers to this question. Pierre Menard is said to be, above all, a parodic figure of Borges himself (his bibliography reveals writings, readings, and even obsessions in common), but he is also said to be his father (this same bibliography strangely resembles that of Jorge Borges, the frustrated writer). But might he be someone else, Paul Valéry for example, a symbolist in his youth with meridional origins, like Menard, in a ruthless parody of the French literary milieu that Borges would come to know? That we could continue to cite other names if we wanted to goes without saying. Why not evoke the historical Pierre Menard (because there was an actual Pierre Menard, a doctor, a professor of psychology, and an author of books on psychotherapy and graphology, also with meridional origins, who lived from 1880 to 1952). To dig deeper into the question, we could even refer to two novels published in France, *Une vie de Pierre Ménard* by Michel Lafon (2008) and *La vraie vie de Pierre Menard, ami de Borges* by René Ventura (2009), or to the works of Pierre Menard, the penname of a French writer born in 1969 with a copious bibliography . . .

It is useless to insist on the detective game. The question does not require a response, but that doesn't mean it's not important; it does in fact shed light on a very important element of the writing process: the use of indexical coding, the multiplication of dissimulated explanations and veiled references, and consequently, the instability or even variability of interpretations of Borges's texts that can be put forth. If the son is first a reader, the strength of the filial position that blurs the codes, identities, and convictions also manifests itself in the question of meaning and in the textual strategies that either help or hinder any potential deciphering.

The mechanism concerns the plot—namely the ambiguities or hidden information (who's who, who does what and why)—and the bibliographical references (who is cited and with what intention), as well as at the other extreme, an inquiry as obsessive as it is melancholic into the meaning of the Universe. The three spheres, the first anecdotic, the second erudite, the third metaphysical, are not, in Borges, very distinct from one another. In "Ibn-Hakam al-Bokhari, Murdered in His Labyrinth" (*The Aleph*), two characters discuss the conditions of a crime that one of them just reported. The one listening is annoyed by the accumulation of enigmas that he senses in the presentation of the facts: "'Please—let's not multiply the mysteries,' he said. 'Mysteries ought to be simple. Remember Poe's purloined letter, remember Zangwill's locked room.'" Faced with a crime story, the operational model is presented as that of the enigmatic detective story, two precursors of which are cited (Poe and Zangwill) along with the emblematic Conan Doyle and his clairvoyant Sherlock Holmes. The example also concerns the metaphysical component, as in the same passage of the story cited above, the friend criticized for excessive enigmas in his story replies, "'Or complex,' volleyed Dunraven. 'Remember the Universe.'"[2]

In reading this exchange we cannot help but think that the great number of Borges's texts that ponder the true name of god and his miraculous value are not far from the *whodunit?* governing traditional detective stories. Sometimes the levels get mixed up, as in one of his detective stories, "Death and the Compass" (*Fictions*), in which the investigation of crimes is superimposed on the announcement of this "hidden name of God," a question dear to a certain branch of Judaism. Finding a quantified, supernatural, and in the end, inconceivable answer—finding this name—is equivalent to giving meaning to what precedes, as is the case in detective stories when mysterious crimes, whose circumstances and actors we have followed throughout the story, are finally elucidated thanks to the explanation of the investigator and the identification of the assassin.

For nothing in Borges seems to be the left to chance; everything refers, we feel, to unexpected content. Taking that into account, we can also consider that there is a secular perception of certain conceptions of sacred writings like that of the Bible or the Koran. Borges's interpretation of Léon Bloy (in "The Mirror of Enigmas"), implies that the writer's stance was comparable to that of Jewish cabalists who based their activity on the idea that "a work dictated by the Holy Spirit was an absolute text: in other words, a text in which the collaboration of chance is calculable at zero"; as a result, "nothing can be contingent in the work of an infinite intelligence."[3] Borges therefore vertiginously associates this semantic overdetermination of texts, this model for the proliferation of meaning, powerful though in the end undecipherable, with the mechanisms of coding and interpretation specific to the detective novel. In Borges's plots, there are not only confrontations, battles, and assassinations, there is also something to discover, someone to accuse; a considerable number of guilty perpetrators belatedly uncovered that move about his narrative world. In the realm of the son, we have seen, there is fault, accident, atonement, rebirth; in the plots, there are traitors, cowards, criminals, and redemptions. Or better, there is an obsession with doublets and oppositions, not only that of father/son and original/rewriting, but also those that incarnate moral figures as well as the criminal ones—master/disciple, infamous/virtuous, coward/hero—figures that are often either inversed or superimposed. In Borges, the traitor and the hero are the same person ("Theme of the Traitor and the Hero," *Fictions*), the victim is found to be the guilty one ("The Shape of the Sword," *Fictions*), the assassin dies before his victim who is the real assassin ("Ibn-Hakam al-Bokhari, Murdered in His Labyrinth," *The Aleph*), and the coward manages to change the past and to die a hero ("The Other Death," *The Aleph*). Meaning and fault are the two passions of the melancholic son, and they are therefore abundantly explored.

These variants reveal the performativity of the detective genre in these stories. Again in "Ibn-Hakam al-Bokhari," we find the following comment on the victim who turns out to be the true assassin: "Such metamorphoses, you will tell me, are classic artifices of the genre—conventions that the reader insists be followed."[4] Enigma, inversions, metamorphoses that distort the identity of the guilty and at the same time the meaning of everything, thereby become part of a convention, a code to respect. This operation, I repeat, goes amply beyond the many plots built upon the foundations of the detective genre.

So, "The universe, *whodunit?*," Borges seems to ask, both accusatory and fearful.

Meaning, That Elegant Hope

Be that as it may, his relationship to the detective novel is intense and regular. A great reader of this literature, Borges often makes reference to it in his essays and conferences (Poe, Conan Doyle, and Chesterton are cited). For him, the detective novel offers above all a formal conception of the story; it is foreign to any form of psychology and is conceived of as a game of intelligence. Yet this relatively rigid structure would be destabilized in his fiction.

Moreover, as mentioned above, the genre implies a way of reading. Borges advances the hypothesis that Edgar Allan Poe not only created the detective novel, "he subsequently created the reader of detective fiction."[5] It goes without saying that this affirmation contains a programmatic scope: creating a genre is inventing a reader, which is a bit like what he does with his erudite, metaphysical, compartmentalized, and polysemic detective fictions. For not only does he theorize about the position of the reader, placing him or her on a level equivalent to that of the author; he also defines the reader's mode of operation through specific writing practices: if there is an ideal reader of his texts, he or she is presented in the form of a detective. The image of the son is that of a writer-reader, he who writes thanks to what has already happened and to what has already been written; the function of the reader that results from this is both specific and particularly powerful. Finally, the third trait deduced from the previous affirmations is that he expands on the detective novel's fields of reference, going from plots that focus on a crime and its resolution to philosophical conjectures: the intelligibility of the real is interpreted in terms of readability.[6]

Furthermore, it should be noted that Borges played an important role in this field as editor of a collection of detective novels and creator, with Adolfo Bioy Casares, of *El Séptimo Círculo* (The seventh circle) in 1945, an series that got its name from nothing less than *The Divine Comedy* and specialized in Anglo-Saxon authors (Borges and Bioy Casares managed the translation and publication of the first 120 volumes of this pioneer collection in the Spanish language). We can therefore say that he was one of the precursors of the "educated" reading and writing of this type of story; indeed, during the second half of the twentieth century, a myriad of writers would adopt the framework of the detective story as a starting point for formally ambitious and aesthetically sophisticated books (consider *The Erasers* by Robbe-Grillet, for example). Borges also wrote detective stories, again in collaboration with Bioy Casares, that describe the cases solved by one Isidro Parodi, whose name announces the parodic and even frankly humorous dimension of the stories told (*Six Problems for Don Isidro Parodi* was published in 1942; later, other co-written detective stories would be published). Additionally, as I have already pointed out, a certain number of his short stories adopt the narrative model of this genre, sometimes inserting surprising reversals and deviations into it. In "Death and the Compass" (*Fictions*), the real investigator is the criminal, and the victim the detective; in "Emma Zunz" (*The Aleph*), the facts that justify the crime and constitute the protagonist's motive are fabricated by her, voluntarily, before the assassination even takes place; in "The Garden of Forking Paths" (*Fictions*), the protagonist, a spy during the First World War, commits murder in order to provide the forces he works for with a name—Albert, which is the name of the victim but also of a French city; in "The Man on the Threshold" (*The Aleph*), a contemporary crime seems to repeat an old one and the secret is known to all the inhabitants of the city, except to the detective narrator.

A particularly clear example of the ambitious use of this narrative pattern can be found in "Tlön, Uqbar, Orbis Tertius." Let us return to this text, a model short story in which an alternative universe, built upon the presuppositions of idealist metaphysics and on the history of Western thought, unfolds. But the plot also reproduces a variation of the detective story and of a genre known to be "minor." If on one hand, there is a Genesis in this text (in the form of a parallel cosmogony in which we follow the conditions and the effects of the emergence of another world) and an Apocalypse (at the end of the text, the narrator affirms "The world will be Tlön" [81] which is equivalent to the destruction of our world as we know it), its sequence of events takes on the form of a mystery and resolution, inviting us to read it as a system of potentially telling clues.

A *mise en abyme* of this mode of functioning can be found in the first few paragraphs of the story when two characters called Borges and Bioy discuss their writing project for a detective story: "We had lost all track of time in a vast debate over the way one might go about composing a first-person novel whose narrator would omit or distort things and engage in all sorts of contradictions, so that a few of the book's readers—a very few—might divine the horrifying or banal truth" (68). This announcement induces a way of reading that is cautious, that might seek to find contradictions, to reveal omitted or disfigured facts, and that might lead to an extraordinary ("atrocious") or minimal ("banal") discovery. Yet the story ends with a revelation that could not be more transcendental—the imminent destruction of the world as we know it.

Just after announcing this project, on the first page of the story, a fortuitous find is made, an error in an edition of *The Anglo-American Cyclopaedia*: certain copies contain extra pages that exceed the alphabetical framework presented in one of the volumes, in which an imaginary country called Uqbar is presented. The discovery of this anomaly triggers a series of speculations aiming to explain it, as well as a significant bibliographical investigation; later, other mysterious texts come into being (their arrivals can be equated to the other types of crimes that sometimes occur in detective novels). Finally, in a postscript, the narrator, taking on the role of a scholarly Sherlock Holmes, offers up a story giving the conditions, circumstances, and impact of the creation of Tlön by a secret society. So there is a "crime" perceived as an incomprehensible disorder (the entry added to certain copies of an encyclopedia), an investigation that leads to the deciphering of clues and confrontations with other "crimes" (an entire volume of an encyclopedia "Tlön" is found), and finally, an organized explanation of the events that occurred before the main action of the text took place.

Although the pattern appears to resemble that of a detective novel, an important difference must be highlighted: not everything is resolved. If, as reader-detectives, we dive back into the text, we would find that there remain many unsolved mysteries and many contradictions in the story, just as "Borges" and "Bioy" desired for the initial project. But most of all, the clarification does not have the effect of a return to order nor of a victory of reason over the incomprehensible; evil and chaos triumph. The most obvious interpretation of the story, which posits Tlön as an image of our world, does not provide a reassuring explanation of any kind along with it; on the contrary, it increases the fantastic dimension and therefore the worrisome aspect of the story: our world is already full of delirium, a totalitarian, nightmarish fiction (after all, one could certainly think that in 1940). In this sense, the moral, reassuring, normative aspect of the detective novel disappears in favor of a nihilist vision of man, society, and the universe.

Interpretation functions here to accentuate the arbitrary nature of our world. More generally, meaning becomes the object of a quest; it is the aim of a consistent and bibliographical trajectory that shifts the question of the identity of the guilty onto meaning itself. Borges's texts multiply references, enumerate a wide variety of examples quite distant from one another, and delimit a stable thirst for knowledge without ever actually managing to *provide* the knowledge sought. Often, investigation takes the form of a series of cross-correlated readings (the typical enumerations of names and historical periods that punctuate Borgesian ideas), transforming reading into an adventure, a story, a solving of mysteries. The librarian of the "Library of Babel," surrounded by an infinite number of books that explain everything and nothing, after trying to uncover some kind of organization, whatever it may be, in the merciless geometry of the Library, describes the situation in the following way: "If an eternal traveler should journey in any direction, he would find after untold centuries that the same volumes are repeated in the same disorder—which, repeated, becomes order: the Order. My solitude is cheered by that elegant hope."[7]

It would not be unreasonable to see here an allegory for reading, one that tells us that reading is an endless movement through a library. Meandering through the work of Borges to the point of brushing up against eternity might, who knows—it is merely an "elegant hope"—allow us to decipher an Order. In hopes of the realization of this utopia, loss is imaginary, hence the melancholy, and Order is nonexistent, hence the investigation. The question of meaning, of the name, of interpretation, is constantly raised; it is entirely central but remains unanswered, or without any possible answer but the quest itself. At the center of the hermeneutical labyrinth, there are consistent movements, the erasure of meaning, and in the end, there is only one subject, the world as a whole, a subject that attempts to be universal; at the center there is nothing, or there is nothing but the figure of Borges and his writing, both, by definition, ambiguous and polysemic. In other words, Borges is meaning, in a way.

Imminent Revelation

A commentary on an essay from *Other Inquisitions*, "The Wall and the Books," will now allow us to illustrate the unique perspective created by this son-reader on the link between meaning and aesthetics. The text is the first one in the book, a position that, as we have already seen in other cases, implies emphasis. It is one of Borges's most well known and most quoted essays.

"The Wall and the Books" has a clear structure: in the first two paragraphs a dilemma is presented, a matter of logic as well as of affect; in the third, several potential solutions to the problem are discussed; and in the fourth, a conclusion that doesn't solve the problem, but displaces it, is provided. The terms of the problem are formulated in the following way: "I read, a few days ago, that the man who ordered the building of the almost infinite Chinese Wall was that first Emperor, Shih Huang Ti, who also decreed the burning of all the books that had been written before his time."[8] This information contains, according to Borges, a contradiction: the two operations—the construction of an extraordinary monument, and the destruction of another, the library—are fundamentally opposed. In learning of these facts, he says, he felt both unexplainable satisfaction and concern; the "notes" that we will now read attempt to "investigate the reasons for that emotion." Although the problem concerns an interpretation of History (what might justify this immense and simultaneous construction and deconstruction?), the objective here is to understand its effects on a given reader. Moreover, he immediately affirms that historically, "there is nothing mysterious about these two measures" (344): the question of meaning surpasses the realm of the factual as well as any predictable explanations. After all, "burning books and erecting fortifications are the usual occupations of princes" (344); only the scale of Shih Huang Ti's action distinguishes it from any other. However, he goes on, how can we understand that someone would still want to build an empire, like we plant a garden? And how is it conceivable that "the most traditional of races renounce the memory of its past, mythical or real" (344)?

The lengthy third paragraph presents itself as the story of an investigation in that it comes back to specific moments of speculation and of reading. Several potential explanations for the facts are then enumerated, one after the other, but without solving the mystery, as the interpretations given never manage to convince Borges—and his readers even less so. Some are psychological: Shih Huang Ti destroyed the library because he wanted to hide the books about the infamy of his mother and in proceeding to do so, repeated the actions of a king in Judea (kill all the children in order to kill one child.) Others suggest a desire for immortality: "the wall in space and the bonfire in time were magic barriers intended to stop death" (345). Another reason considered is the demonstration of the desire to be first in everything, the absolute founder, including of language, by giving things their "true name": "Perhaps the Emperor wanted to recreate the beginning of time" (345). And still others question the order of events, first the destruction, then the construction, or the opposite: we would have, accordingly, "the image of a king who began by destroying and then resigned himself to conserving; or the image of a disillusioned king who destroyed what he had once defended," "dramatic" conjectures lacking, he affirms, any historical foundation. In the end, the wall might only have been "a metaphor" through which Shih Huang Ti aimed to condemn those who loved the past to build a wall, in other words, a task "as vast as the past, as stupid and as useless" (345). Or perhaps he destroyed the books knowing that they were superfluous since they taught just what the universe or the conscience of each man and woman teaches; or maybe he built the wall because he knew that empire was perishable. These affirmations lead to one last speculation that trumps all the others: "Perhaps the burning of the libraries and the building of the wall are acts that in some secret way erase each other" (346).

There is obviously much to say about each of these proposed hypotheses, but let us limit ourselves to drawing attention to the fact that these different answers point, above all, to complexity and reveal an unavoidable contradiction. In expanding the possibilities, the investigation, rather than solving the problem, extends its terms and therefore prolongs it. The final suggestion can even be read as a kind of implosion, as it serves to cancel out the information given in the question stated at the beginning of the essay. The arrival at this proposal implies a certain narrative tension that can be felt: the different explanations are equivalent to the transformation of an initial situation into a resolution. The construction is that of a story, as much in its idea of chronological evolution as in the movements from cause to effect at play in each of the elements that constitute it.

The conclusion that can be drawn from the end of the text displaces the problem by adopting a much more lyrical tone than in the rest of the text. It voids the events—the construction of the wall and the destruction of the library—of their historicity and their circumstances; the coincidence of the two events is reduced to an idea, an opposition between construction and destruction "on an enormous scale." The assessment is situated elsewhere: "the idea is what moves us, quite apart from the speculations it allows" (346). Consequently, there is nothing to be interpreted, or to seek meaning in, even if the entire text respects the imperatives of interpretation and the attribution of meaning. What remains are the emotions felt (satisfaction and concern), which Borges explains in a few vertiginous lines about the arts that aspire to pure form with a relative indifference to meaning but not to feelings. In the final lines, we find one of the most well-known passages that Borges wrote, which brings the question at the beginning of "The Wall and the Books" into the realm of the programmatic and the aesthetic: "Music, states of happiness, mythology, faces worn by time, certain twilights and certain places, all want to tell us something, or have told us something we shouldn't have lost, or are about to tell us something; that imminence of a revelation as yet unproduced is perhaps, the aesthetic fact" (346). Here lies the true revelation: what is sought is the imminence of meaning, the impression of a thickness of meaning, the belief in a utopia of meaning—not some truth, affirmation, or certainty. Aesthetic experience lies in the investigation and in its effects—in other words, in a certain type of reading.

Performative Disbelief

"The Wall and the Books" develops a theory of action within literature. On one hand, the expansion of investigation, the intention to interpret, and the bibliographical journey are seen as an adventure, thought and deduction as dramatic, in the theatrical sense of the term. On the other, we find the explicit affirmation of an indifference to the ultimate meaning of things or perhaps an admission of disbelief in the existence of a meaning to find. In a 1940 essay on Léon Bloy, Borges wrote, "it is doubtful that the world has a meaning; it is more doubtful still, the incredulous will observe, that it has a double and triple meaning."[9] Some years later, in an interview with María Esther Vásquez, Borges comes back to the question:

> I have no theory on the world. Generally speaking, as I used different metaphysical and theological systems to literary ends, readers thought I adhered to these systems, although the only thing I did was take advantage of them for those ends, nothing more. In addition, if I had to define myself, I would say I am agnostic, meaning an individual who doesn't believe that full awareness is possible. Or in any case, as it has been said on many occasions, there is no reason why a cultured man of the twentieth century should be able to understand the universe.[10]

His work appears to be built around this principle of essential unintelligibility.

These remarks could be contested, and they have been by recurrent philosophical readings of his work. The expression "literary ends," which remains, all things considered, enigmatic, is to be underscored ("I used different metaphysical and theological systems to literary ends"). For literature (and writing) is to be found through the exposure of a journey through the library, through logic, through the practice of thought, but this journey merely lays out, deploys, an emotion; the formal exacerbation and logic games always lead to the oneiric, the imaginary, the impossible. On several occasions, he affirmed that literature is a dream: "If literature is a dream (a controlled and deliberate dream, but fundamentally a dream)."[11] In "Nathaniel Hawthorne," the essay from which this quote is taken, he also provides a commentary on a page of Hawthorne's work that seems to him untenable from the vantage point of reason, yet he just as soon adds that pure reason must not interfere with art. Writing means following the logic of "dreams, which have their singular and secret algebra, and in whose ambiguous realm one thing may be many."[12]

As we can observe, Borges borrows writing patterns and logical structures from the detective novel, and the displacements he carries out on these elements, as well as on others (philosophy, history, theology), must not be neglected. He appropriates them in transforming them into the scaffolding of a powerful dream, which is why the question of meaning (metaphysical and detective-style at the same time) leads to the imminence of an ever-promised revelation that is never accomplished. Nonetheless, the melancholic process of questioning the meaning of the world and of works of art without offering any answers leaves an extraordinary potentiality open to interpretation, which, in a way, goes against the skeptical assumptions of Borges's beginnings. Reading Borges is an adventure into meaning, doing so implies the constant confrontation with clues, bibliographical hints, logical suppositions that mobilize endless hermeneutic activity. Matters of knowledge and meaning, more than of characters, are in a way transferred to the receptors, who become the "very rare readers" capable of discovering reality, be it "atrocious or banal," according to the *incipit* of "Tlön."

The extraordinary posterity of these texts might not be foreign to the plasticity of the readings for which this process allows. This would explain why throughout the history of the reception of his work, readers have found different content, depending on the historical or cultural context and on the knowledge of each individual: some have found in the pages of Borges illustrations of quantum physics, and others generalized theories on alchemy, to provide two extreme and opposed examples. More seriously, Borges has been considered the paradigm of the neobaroque movement of Latin American literature, as a theorist of the death of the author and of generalized intertextuality, and as the precursor of postmodernity and the founder of world literature. His lifework has been studied through the lens of disciplines as diverse as theology, philosophy, and literary theory, not to mention mathematics and architecture.

Borges obliges his readers, they who arrive after the writing but are placed on the same level as the author, to interpret, to reason, and in the end, to feel. The reading of his texts conveys a conviction that is quite difficult to define, a feeling of being intelligent, almost as smart as him. Yet according to a very famous sentence included in "Notes on (in Search of) Bernard Shaw," it is in the reception itself that originality and the distance between different literary objects is played out: "one literature differs from another, either before or after it, not so much because of the text as for the manner in which it is read."[13] Consequently, and to adopt an aphoristic form so commonly used by Borges, we might conclude that Borges is, above all, a way of reading.

CHAPTER 6

The Library

Tradition, Betrayal, and Transgression

My memory, sir, is like a garbage heap.

"Funes, His Memory," 1942[1]

IN 2010, THE Argentine National Library published a homage to Borges, its director for eighteen years, in the form of an atypical book: *Borges, libros y lecturas* [Borges, books and readings], a systematic but not exhaustive account of the notes written by Borges in the margins of the works that composed a great portion of his personal library, left to the institution by the writer upon his retirement in 1973. For various reasons administrative and political, this archive had been dispersed, requiring meticulous work to reconstruct only a portion of it. Among the nine hundred thousand works in the National Library catalog, around a thousand books were identified at the time as coming from Borges's donation; the notes left by Borges from about half of those thousand were then transcribed. This included commentary, quotes, and some personal information (friendships, romance, victories, failures, professional activities, plans, and tables of contents of textbooks), which is why these pages can be read as a kind of writer's journal. The result is an imposing volume, the most surprising of the author's books published posthumously.

The origin of the quotes present in the edited volume, the reformulations, the source of this or that idea, can, in many cases, be traced and identified, and the notes clearly show that reading was a direct catalyst for writing. The erudite proliferation manifested in the published texts and the accent put on reading as an action equivalent to creation are, thus, not mere textual effects: they correspond to his actual practices. *Borges, libros y lecturas* therefore allows us to confirm the axiom according to which reading is a writerly operation.

In any event, the illustration is powerful: Borges is a writer-reader, a writer who, through imaginary iconography, instead of a pen, might carry a pencil in his hand to underline, circle an idea, or draw a line between two authors. Without a doubt, up to a certain period, he read a tremendous amount, but his operations with reading—highlighting certain traits, certain constants, certain episodes, certain unexpected similarities—were arguably more important. Writing is not only reading; it is also underling, making visible, comparing, making lists of quotes. Ultimately, on a symbolic level, the anecdote of Borges's writing being present but lost in the archives of the Argentine National Library is not anodyne. His writing can be found in the margins of books in a library and, accordingly, in the periphery of universal culture.

This description of the book allows for three major traits of Borges's relationship to erudition to be established: first, its hyperbolic nature that has at its horizon—or as an ambition or ideal—the whole of lettered culture. Secondly, its function in writing as a starting point or catalyst for creation. And finally, the transgressive operations that characterize this lettered appropriation, its readings in combination that delegitimize hierarchies and relocate traditional centers of knowledge to the peripheries of the world.

The main ideas in the content of this library mobilized behind the scenes in these texts are well known. The library included on the one hand, Western philosophy (the Greeks, the English idealists, and Schopenhauer are recurrent references), and on the other, different facets of theology: the Bible, the heretic traditions of Christianity (like the Gnostics and the apocryphal Gospels), Jewish and Muslim metaphysics, and Buddhist beliefs (in an essay from *Other Inquisitions*, Borges speculates that "every educated man is a theologian";[2] he could have made the same statement about philosophers). And finally, we must cite the presence of works of Western and Oriental mythologies, without necessarily drawing a clear line between these two forms of thought. These are theories that make hermeneutics and the explanation of the world, whatever it may be, their foundations, or that turn them into a way of telling, as in the case of the mythological story. We have a literary library that is arbitrary and heterogeneous, despite the strong presence of Anglophone literatures alongside Spanish classics, *The Divine Comedy*, and certain moments in Germanic or French literatures (Valéry and Verlaine, for example are recurrent in his referential universe).

But more than the content of the catalog of this intimate library, what attracts our attention is the hyperbolic usage of it. Two examples clearly demonstrate this proliferation. First, the essay "On the Cult of Books" takes us on a journey through the history of the perception of books as sacred objects. Straight away, Borges compares Homer and *The Odyssey* to Mallarmé (considering them as belonging to two different "theologies"); then Cervantes, Bernard Shaw, Pythagoras, Plato, Clement of Alexandria, the Gospel according to John, Saint Augustin, Lucien of Samosata, Flaubert, Henry James, James Joyce, the Koran, the Old Testament, the Jewish Cabalist tradition, Francis Bacon, Thomas Browne, Carlyle, and Léon Bloy are cited at random. The list only includes the names mentioned, but other references are most certainly implicit in this four- or five-page text.

With regard to fiction, one story stands out: "Tlön, Uqbar, Orbis Tertius" and its invention of a world built around references to literary history, philosophy, and theology. The story is saturated with indexes of this type; without attempting to interpret them and in limiting ourselves to explicit mentions, we can list the police novel, Andreä, De Quincey, Berkeley, Xul Solar, Ultraism and the Avant-gardes, Meinong, Spinoza, Shakespeare, Saint Augustin, Russell, Hume, Zeno of Elea, Schopenhauer, Quevedo, and Browne, for example.

This vertiginous list of authors and works in Borges's works—some iconoclasts have insinuated—might be the result of a certain snobbery (we read in a story from *The Aleph*, "The Zahir," that snobbery is "the sincerest of Argentine passions"[3]). What is remarkable is that this accumulation aims for totality: any reference from the entire library and any time period can potentially be mentioned, thanks to Borges's unexpected comparisons. In this respect, the text functions like other Borgesian listings that intend to suggest totality. These heterogeneous, vertiginous enumerations are a form often used to communicate the hypermnesia of Funes or to convey, with precision, the content of the Library of Babel.

Here like elsewhere, Borges's imagination borders on delusions of grandeur: not only does the library tend toward totality, but the book is also projected in its ideal form capable of finishing off all other books or of containing them, just as time often tends toward eternity (there is even a *History of Eternity*, let us remember), iniquity is universal (*A Universal History of Iniquity*), spaces open onto infinity, in the stairway leading to any basement in Buenos Aires hides the Aleph (the point from which the universe and the world can be observed with concurrent, superhuman completeness), immortality can be found on almost any street corner, and today's events merely update the events that have been repeating themselves since the beginning of time . . .

A Narrative Syntax

Erudition is a writing technique in itself, a source of fables and imagination, a machine for producing stories and effects; this use of culture is textual "syntax," that is, a formal mechanism implying the integration of other books and other authors, as well as the shifting of their intentionality or their meaning.[4] In the epilogue of *Other Inquisitions*, Borges admits that one of the dominant tendencies of the book that we have just read is that of evaluating "religious or philosophical ideas on the basis of their aesthetic worth and even for what is singular and marvelous about them."[5] This explains why we often attribute to Borges a sentence by Gérard Genette that says that the modern form of the fantastic is erudition, an erroneous attribution that is, in itself, quite Borgesian.

This observation explains why the most recurrent description of Borges depicts him as a librarian writer, or on another level, a writer whose writing is based only on other books; an apocryphal writer, making use of false references, inventing incredible languages, with an imagination elicited through erudition. In one of the first assessments of the phenomenon, a review of the first edition of *The Garden of Forking Paths* (in the first part of *Fictions*) (1941), Adolfo Bioy Casares describes a "literature of literature and of thought" and salutes what, for him, creates a "new genre" of story or what, at least "renews and expands on the narrative genre."[6]

More than forty years later, Italo Calvino—as it has already been mentioned—would credit Borges with "the last great invention of a new literary genre in our time."[7] Faced with the impossibility of writing the book that we would like to write, it is a matter of imagining that such a thing exists, and of building a story around its description. This mechanism is the catalyst for an approach to stories, in that it doubles or multiplies "its own space through the medium of other books belonging to a real or imaginary library, whether they be classical, erudite, or merely invented." As in a game of mirrors, "a literature raised to the second power," "literature that is like the extraction of the square root of itself," a "potential literature" is born.[8]

In a 1927 text, Borges had already sketched out a particular relationship to books and to the imagination that they invoke: "Our indolence speaks of classical books, eternal books. If only some eternal book existed, primed for our enjoyment and whims, no less inventive in the populous morning as in the secluded night, oriented toward all hours of the world."[9] Tempted like Mallarmé by the Book, haunted by the utopic form of the perfect, transformative book, Borges paves his way by multiplying fables on the existence and the writing of an impossible book; the mechanism is not without connection to a certain melancholy that turns the imaginary loss of an object never possessed into a mode of possession. In this way, Borges gets as close as possible to this ideal book.

For the desire for a superior book is underlying in all these imaginary books that traverse his works, despite the justification for these inventions provided in the prologue of *The Garden of Forking Paths* that attributes them to laziness, reason, and incapacity.[10] This desire is manifested in the major apparatuses that give way to the form of an encyclopedia and therefore of a fictitious totality or, in its minimalist version, to the sacred writing of a god to be deciphered (as in "The Writing of the God," in *The Aleph*, for example), or to a single line that contains an entire palace ("Parable of the Palace," *The Maker*). From general inauthenticity and the deformation of sources to rewriting that reappropriates the texts of others, these practices all have their origins, as it has been said, in *A Universal History of Iniquity*, the book in which the "lives" recounted are outrageously deformed with respect to the historical truth, or at least estranged from the sources used. This first exercise in fictional erudition reveals another aspect: the reckless and unlawful side of these encyclopedic practices. Authors are invented; words are confiscated; there is plagiarism, fabulation, and recycling of the stories of mass culture (the series, the action or adventure film). In this "iniquitous" context, the relationship to the texts of others (to the spiritual belongings of others), is marked by theft, lies, and dissimulation: these are quotes that we could call renegade.

The specifics of this extreme case are at stake in every subsequent reappropriation and erudite allusion. The first implication of this utilitarian side of erudition is that invoking the library and the Classics does not imply their authority nor the legitimizing force that the mention of such traditions and great names usually has. The act of appropriating a prestigious name or a well-written expression for literary purposes is subversive in itself: the library is treated as a source of stories and not as a catalog of Masters.

The brief story "Ragnarök" (included in *The Maker*) illustrates this practice well. The story narrates a dream about the intrusion of two pagan gods into the middle of a meeting at the College of Philosophy and Letters in Buenos Aires, while a group is getting ready to elect "the authorities." A dreaming Borges is among those present, when suddenly, "Here they come! . . . The gods! the gods!" Indeed, the gods "were returning after a banishment of many centuries";[11] Janus, Thoth and other mythological creatures took to the podium of the auditorium and "haughtily" accepted the men's homage. But after this triumphant arrival of the gods, who pretended to be "the authorities" meant to be elected at the meeting, the situation changes. The decadence of the divinities abruptly becomes obvious: they are no longer haloed with the grandeur of their pre-Christian and pre-Muslim past; their "Olympian" race finds itself degraded, mixed in with "the sparse beard of a mulatto or a Chinaman"; their clothing was "of criminal luxury of the Underworld's gambling dens and houses of ill repute."[12] The authorities selected from the most glorious traditions of the West and of antiquity are called upon, but they have become bastards, impure gods, for they have incorporated the mixed blood of the Americas and the habits of the ghettos of Buenos Aires. It is only after being met with enthusiasm that the divinities turn vicious. Without hesitating, Borges and the others get out their "heavy revolvers" and "exultantly" kill the gods.

This is the fate of the authorities of high culture: to be quoted, transformed, and destroyed in a single gesture of veneration and irreverence.

Nonetheless, although the call upon great figures might therefore cast doubt upon, "Argentinize," and even sometimes destroy them, there is a certain Classicism at work in Borges. He believes in the permanence of forms and in the transhistoricity of literary themes, all the while defending the capacity to innovate and to propose variations that might alter a given inherited tradition from within.

But this same Classicism sometimes becomes mere prose. Borges keeps his distance from the prestige of erudition, suggesting that the latter can be false, that it can be merely fiction improvised to serve a text. For we notice that these quotes are not part of a coherent system, one that might respect hierarchies and belongings; in mixing well-known, unknown, and invented quotes and references, he tends to favor the suppression of the delimitation of a culture. However, this suppression does not function through direct condemnation (as the avant-garde movement did), but rather through exaggeration and parody of the usual methods of lettered culture, introducing faults that destabilize the whole.[13]

Even the dialogue entertained with tutelary figures is based on appropriation, deformation, and decontextualization (with respect to a time period or national affiliation). Furthermore, the repeated recovery of secondary, minor, or unknown writers functions in the same way; this reclaiming becomes the token of a kind of "post-Borgesian" fame, as is the case for Evaristo Carriego who, today, would be but a forgotten name in a dusty anthology of Argentine poetry had it not been for Borges's powerful intervention. Indeed, it is probably not by chance that Borges dedicated several poems to unknown and minor poets.[14]

The best examples of this systematic avoidance of the authorities are the direct quotes that Borges uses and abuses in his prologues and epilogues. In these texts, Borges systematically takes refuge in the quote or the analogy between his intentions, opinions, and ideas and those of such and such famous predecessor. Often, the result gives the impression of a collage: it appears as though Borges were incapable of thinking or stating anything without resorting to the words of another. Yet, in the end, the great figures of Western culture either agree with Borges or end up putting forth ideas similar to Borges's and therefore fully prefiguring and preparing the way for him. The conversion of the emblems of knowledge and the values of culture into fiction, personal imagination, and subjective discourse therefore explain the fact that an illegitimate—iniquitous—practice of erudition could be evoked.

The different characteristics of this careless conception of erudition and of the imaginary practice of the scholarly reference allow us to sketch out a certain posture with regard to the inherited library. We find creative marginality or emphasis on the conventions that are the basis for a classic, an authority, a tradition, as well as a paradoxical dialectic between parricidal submission, respective destruction, and the worship of the sacrilegious. For Borges, being traditional involves accentuating newness and reorganizing the history of thought around his own figure, and the library around his belief system. In that way, the author imagined himself as a founder, even at a moment in his life when his heroic traits had been obscured by respect and modesty; in calling upon existing traditions through the library, he displaces them, and as such, founds a tradition. His position is of course ambivalent as he goes from worship to aggressivity; each step of the way, he recognizes his filiations, but his approaches and literary practices tend to muddle them. He is both on the inside and on the outside—his originality in the *orillas*, that we emphasized earlier—but he can also be seen as a docile parricide, a cursed heir, a clairvoyant blindman, a powerful weakling, a fatherless son, a destructive creator. The strength of Borges's relationship to tradition is the result of its ambiguity and polyvalence.

The Argentine Writer and Tradition

At the beginning of the 1950s and under a Peronist government that led to the reinforcement of nationalist sentiment, Borges gave a conference transcribed and included in the late editions of his book *Discussion*, "The Argentine Writer and Tradition," which would undoubtedly become one of the author's most quoted and most commented on texts. He tackles head on the question of the tradition from which the Argentine writer should write: a national tradition made up of themes and spaces considered to be specific to Argentina, a Spanish tradition derived from the colonial history of the country, or perhaps a European tradition that takes into account the close relationships weaved with the continent? The question might seem outdated in our era of cultural globalization, but it was not at all at the end of the 1940s; in fact, it occupied an important role in the building of national Latin American literatures when the debate was often over the type of connections that should be established with the cultural centers of the world. In the quest for an identifiable originality with which comes an identity, a certain perception of nature—as a differentiating trait, and in the end, as a distinctive essence of reality in itself—was a frequent response. The most powerful translation of this idea would be the postulate of a "fantastic reality" or of "magic realism" specific to Latin America; the image of the sub-continent, or Alejo Carpentier and Gabriel García Márquez, or of Miguel Angel Asturias, would be strongly influenced by the presence of the extraordinary, the irrational, the outrageous inherent in this vision.

The quest for literature that might be able to account for, to symbolize, and to sublimate national belonging was therefore on the agenda of the time; the work Borges produced in youth fit well into this context of desire for particularism. And he would come back to this question in the 1940s and 1950s. The political context explained in part his taking a position, although the explicit exposure of his idea of tradition was certainly a more determinant motivation, despite the fact that he was, at the time, in the process of writing the texts considered to be the most "universalist" of his entire work. This clarification was not superfluous: for several decades, Borges would be accused of turning his back on reality, especially on the reality of Argentina, and of preferring useless encyclopedic games to the situation (especially the political situation) in his country and in Latin America that he seemed not to know about. This negative reading is a major phenomenon in his work; it is also, abroad, a reading that exalts, on the contrary, the universal dimension of a writer coming from the outer reaches of the world.

In this text, Borges pretends to take the initial question seriously: how to resolve "the problem of the Argentine writer and tradition"? According to the logical pattern that often governs his texts, he begins by presenting the potential solutions to the "problem" before exposing his opinion on the subject. The first response, discussed in detail, is that of nationalism, according to which tradition can be found in the authors of the nineteenth century who sang of the *gaucho* and the pampa; the model to follow might be the quest for Argentine specificities. Of course, he diametrically opposes this option, contesting the supposed correspondence between human reality and its textual image and emphasizing the artifice entailed in systemically seeking to include elements of "local color." He then indulges in presenting the English or American influences on his "landmark" books of literary nationalism.

In that regard, he puts forth a comparison, an erudite one of course, that would have extraordinary resonance due to the number of times that it would be cited. Building on *The History of the Decline and Fall of the Roman Empire* by Gibbon, who observes at one point or another that "in the Arab book par excellence, the Koran, there are no camels." Borges interprets this observation with radicality: "I believe that if there were ever any doubt as to the authenticity of the Koran, this lack of camels would suffice to prove that it is Arab."[15] We perceive the paradox: not mentioning what might seem to be most "typically" Arab is proof of belonging to Arabia. Camels being part of his daily reality, there would have been no reason for Mohammed to consider them particular; he was "unconcerned: he knew he could be Arab without camels." Borges draws from this a first conclusion: "I believe that we Argentines can be like Mohammed; we can believe in the possibility of being Argentine without abounding in local color" (424), for local color is but a voluntarist gesture of self-affirmation, foreign to any kind of authenticity. The comparison and the conclusion are provocative but very telling due, among other things, to the indirect perspective chosen to make reference to horses (horses that hide behind these camels in the Arabian desert and that are the iconographical trait of the *gaucho*). Of course, this shift of the problem, through the introduction of a distant cultural sphere, is not lacking in irony.

Then Borges quickly reviews two other responses (the Spanish tradition and the lack of tradition in a "new" country, which would be favorable to invention) before going on to explain his own view and to raise doubt as to the actual existence of the problem at hand. His opinion is that the tradition of the Argentines "is the whole of Western culture" and that they have an "even greater right" to this tradition, regarded as a single entity, than the "inhabitants of one Western nation or another may have" (426). The reasoning behind this obviously incongruous statement is another comparison, this time between the situation of Argentines and European culture on the one hand, and of that of the Jews and the Irish on the other, a comparison accompanied by a potential explanation for the creative prowess of the latter within European culture. The idea is that Argentines (or Jews, or the Irish), are part of European culture without having any particular devotion to one nation or another. They belong to this culture, but they may also be, in a way, exterior to it: this exteriority is what ensures their enhanced ability to innovate. We see a second paradox emerge: it is because the Argentines are not entirely part of what makes up their culture, or because they are, to a certain extent, exterior to it, that they have the right to it, and that they can be particularly original in their creations based on it. This situation therefore allows them to "take on all the European subjects, take them on without superstition and with an irreverence that can have, and already has had, fortunate consequences" (426). The statement is clear both on the wager on universality and on the erudite methods that Borges himself had perfected in the 1940s, methods used "without superstition" and "with irreverence."

After these programmatical affirmations, Borges concludes his text by deconstructing the assumptions of the discussion and therefore of the problem of tradition in itself. His skepticism relates to two points. First, from a general standpoint, he mentions the error of assuming that intentions and plans that precede writing have any importance; as proof, he turns to the example of *Gulliver's Travels*, the book in which Swift wanted to "raise an indictment against mankind and instead left behind a children's book" (427). The second point is a negation of all forms of national determinism: "Everything we Argentine writers do felicitously will belong to Argentine tradition, in the same way that the use of Italian subjects belongs to the tradition of England through the work of Chaucer and Shakespeare" (426). From two things, we can conclude one: "either it is our inevitable destiny to be Argentine, in which case we will be Argentine whatever we do, or being Argentine is a mere affectation, a mask" (427). The statement in the end aims to posit the autonomy of creation with respect to any delimitation of what can conceivably be written or not; on the contrary, he believes that "if we lose ourselves in the voluntary dream called artistic creation, we will be Argentine" (427). Here like elsewhere, his youthful heroism is at work.

Borges's stance is double-sided, which, in a way, puts an end to the debate and places his projects at the center of what can therefore be called Argentine literature. He defends a lateral cosmopolitanism or, if you will, an Argentinity defined as a way of reading

Western culture, which indirectly gives "national" legitimacy to the texts that he himself was in the process of writing at the time. At the same time, he turns his back on all essentialist visions of tradition and denies the existence of the problem, but supposes the possibility of belonging from the margins, the suburbs, and the *orillas* of Western culture. His version of modernity is peripheral and destabilizes culture as a fixed monument.

A Universal Periphery

This series of stances and statements played a major role in the internationalization and modernization of Latin American literatures; what would follow in the history of culture would often prove him right. Nonetheless, these matters (tradition and the relationship between the Argentine margins and great European culture) have not been resolved; we could instead say that they become more complex when we find them in the stories and poems of Borges. They in fact exceed the declarations of principles that deny the problem or advocate for the mere freedom of creation.

Borges, after his creolist youth, continues to be obsessed with the question of belonging and with the role that can be attributed to (or created for) Argentine literature in the world—or the role that can be attributed to his own literature. Once this fact has been established, the use of the quote takes on a new meaning. The phenomenon has more to do with the displacement and appropriation of other cultures than with the mere inclusion of erudite references taken from distant places. In his essays, poems, and especially in his stories, the main events, the great metaphysical questions, and most important pages of Western tradition are adopted and adapted to a new context, namely, the work of the Argentine. For after all, Buenos Aires is where we find the Aleph, that extraordinary cosmic point of view on time and space; it is near Borges that the main events leading to the discovery of Tlön and to the collapse of our world take place; and it is in the Uruguayan pampa that we find Funes, an emblem of the meticulous memory of all cultures. The starting point is indeed the periphery, but it is a periphery devoted to centrality. Borges distributes the cultures of the entire world around himself, around Buenos Aires and around Río de la Plata, a bit like in the world maps that seek to transform our geopolitical views of the world by putting something other than the Atlantic Ocean and the Europe/United States axis in the middle, as a structural point.

In the end, the question is not foreign to other aforementioned aspects of his work; on the one hand, the data is similar to that of paradoxical originality that Borges discovers in rewriting: with respect to tradition, repetition is also what makes the difference. On the other hand, it is by operating with readings that writing happens and, in the case of tradition, reading is to be seen as a translational gesture. At any given moment, the fiction furthest away from Borges's space-time can appear to evoke Argentina (if I write while reading, what I read is always talking about me; I transcribe it onto my own coordinates). And that is how the unlikely geography of some kind of Asian antiquity can resemble this country ("The Circular Ruins"), how a European city whose toponymy is French can oddly remind us of Buenos Aires ("Death and the Compass"), how the building of a Irish national hero in the nineteenth century can illustrate that of the great figures of Latin American independence ("The Theme of the Traitor and the Hero"), how universal iniquity can become a framework in which to introduce the crooks of the suburbs of Buenos Aires (*Universal History of Iniquity*), how the Arabian desert, perceived of as a labyrinth created by Allah, can remind us of an empty pampa, conducive to metaphysical inklings, and according to the established phrase, to "horizonal vertigo" ("The Two Kings and the Two Labyrinths"). The Universal culture mobilized is thus not foreign; it is used to evoke and encode the traditions and realities linked to Argentina. Through these mechanisms of appropriation, another way of being an Argentine writer is defined. Despite their peripheral location and at the same time, these writers become equals to the great names of European culture: they have the right to all subjects, all speculations, all perplexities, and to fables about time. Argentine authors posterior to Borges have understood the upsetting of hierarchies that underlies this operation and have advanced in the same direction (Ricardo Piglia, Juan José Saer, and César Aira, for example).

The phenomenon becomes even more apparent when we consider the counterpart to these scholarly references, namely, the numerous texts of Borges's lifework that prolong the themes of the outskirts of the city and of the pampa. In this sense, the most noble and highest of Western traditions are commingled with *gauchos* and crooks from the slums, as in the story that showcases the interconnected fates of two characters ("Story of the Warrior and the Captive Maiden," *The Aleph*), a barbaric warrior fascinated with the Ravenna of late antiquity and an English woman who chooses to live with Indians. To a certain extent, in the pampa of the nineteenth century, a tragic dilemma is played out that has its roots in history's greatest idiosyncrasies. In "The Plot" (*The Maker*), the expression of a horrified Julius Cesar when he recognizes his adopted son among the assassins ("*Et tu, Brute?*") is repeated, nineteen centuries later, in the southern part of the province of Buenos Aires, from the mouth of a *gaucho* who, as he falls, recognizes one of his godsons among his aggressors and cries out "*Pero, che!*"[16] The expression is informal, but the interjection "*che*" is in fact specific to the Argentine spoken language. There is permanence (from Julius Cesar to the *gaucho*), repetition, and finally, translation. "*Pero, che!*" is equated here to "*Et tu, Brute?*," one of the most famous phrases spoken in Classic European culture.

Let us look at one final example, a late story that depicts a complex network of determinisms and of translations of a major text, one of the Gospels: "The Gospel According to Mark" (included in *El informe de Brodie* [1970; Brodie's report]).[17] It tells the story of a dandy from Buenos Aires, Baltasar Espinosa, who finds himself, after a flood, isolated in a hacienda in the middle of the pampa in the company of a sharecropper and his family, the Gutres. The Gutres are of Scottish and Indian descent (they are *gauchos*). In the house the protagonist finds a Bible in English that belonged to the family, members of which had inscribed, on its last pages, their family history, which comes to an end in 1870 when the Gutres began to forget English. To pass the time, after dinner Espinosa decides to read them "The Gospel according to Mark." And that is how, night after night, he would translate the sacred text into Spanish and, before the silent interest and concentration of his listeners, would be forced to recommence when he arrives at the end, that is, at the passion of the Christ. This reading, this translation of a text that the *gauchos* have had in their blood since their departure from Scotland and their Calvinist past (it is the opinion of the protagonist) leads to a surprising result: the Gutres take the text they heard literally and decide to reenact the Gospel. They crucify Espinosa. As we can see, translation and cultural displacement outline a quite labyrinthic trajectory: the Scots turned *gauchos* (and therefore "barbarians") commit an act of violence that coincides with the space and the time of the action; but they do it by imitating a book in English that was a symbol of national and religious belonging for their ancestors. In the pampa, the passion of the Christ, deformed and displaced, is reenacted. The barbary of the *gauchos* and the Indians is presented as the symmetrical counterpoint to that of the Calvinists or even to that of the myth of the Christians who would martyr a man they would then come to worship.

In this way, Borgesian universalism, so highly lauded and so strongly attacked, is not uniform or coherent; it is a way of situating himself and of defining himself as a writer, first of all, but also a way of defining himself as an Argentine. This type of ambivalence was already present in his youth; in his *Autobiographical Essay*, he explains how, when visiting the Roman ruins of Verona for the first time, the adolescent that he was began to recite *gaucho* poetry in the amphitheater.[18] The superimposition of two cultural spheres was already at work. At the time, he was quoting a great number of European writers, exposing not only his knowledge but also his Argentinity in translating their names: "Lorenzo Stern," "Jorge Bernardo Shaw" or—the effect is quite strange—"Jorge Federico Guillermo Hegel." Then in the important text of this creolist period that is "The Full Extent of My Hope," and after having called for the foundation of a literary Buenos Aires, Borges evokes, as we have said, a specific kind of localism: "*Criollismo* by all means but a *criollismo* that converges with the world and with the individual and with God and with death."[19] A creolism that is also made up of metaphysics and universality. The proposal then seems to reverse itself, for Borges's later version of universalism converses with localism and with Argentina's past, its geography, its history, and its imagination. Universalism is then perceived as a sideways reading that appropriates the cultures of others and transforms them into its own.

The fact that Borges, who was rejected or at least criticized by several generations of readers for his aggressive cosmopolitanism and for his apparent indifference toward the reality of his country, would then become the emblem of Argentine culture to the point of being placed at the heart of its literary system is, without a doubt, proof of the efficiency of his maneuvering of erudition that we have just presented.

CHAPTER 7

Forms of Eternity

... eternity, a game or a spent hope.
A History of Eternity, 1936[1]

THE MAIN HYPOTHESIS of Paul Ricoeur's monumental work *Time and Narrative* is summed up by the author in these terms: "speculation on time is an inconclusive rumination to which narrative activity alone can respond. Not that this activity solves the aporias through substitution. If it does resolve them, it is in a poetical and not a theoretical sense of the word."[2] This significance of the aporias of time for narration is indeed exacerbated in literature, for literature offers imaginative variations, making it possible to escape the limitations of historical time, which is often in conflict with subjective time and phenomenological time.

Borges's work is capable of providing a nearly exhaustive repertoire of these "imaginative variations" that not only revive aporias, they also render them productive. In fiction, the impossibility of conceiving of time is no longer paralyzing.[3] Multiple times, time that flows from the future to the past, the malleability of the past that is susceptible to transformation, time that forks in a decentered labyrinth, cyclical time, immobile or dilated time, demiurgical mastery of all times, legendary times, diverse forms of eternity. This vast domain of fictional proliferation overlaps with erudition—for his rantings on time are the subject of both narrative scenes and insistent philosophical and theological references—as well as with melancholy, the lucid regret that leaves its mark on every self-representation in Borges.

The author identifies the roots of his obsession with time in a kind of revelation in youth that came about, without any apparent reason, during a stroll through Buenos Aires at night, on a street corner unfamiliar to him. It would give rise to a text included in *The Language of the Argentines* (1928) titled "Feeling in Death," part of which was transcribed in *A History of Eternity* (1936). Looking at the simplicity of the landscape before him, the writer has the sudden conviction that he is in a reality thirty years past, which gives him the certainty that he had "made [his] way upstream on the presumptive waters of Time" and that he is now "in possession of the reticent or absent meaning of the inconceivable word eternity." The moment that he experienced was, he imagines, not *like* another moment in the past; it was exactly the same one. "When we can feel this oneness, time is a delusion which the indifference and inseparability of a moment from its apparent yesterday and from its apparent today suffice to disintegrate."[4] The revelation was therefore that of a perceivable eternity: "life is too impoverished not to be immortal."[5]

The Forking of Time

This inkling of eternity and this subjective perception of time would warrant bibliographical investigations, numerous essays, and poems on this subject. They provide one of the writing models for the fantasy stories that insist on multiplicity and superimpose contradictory visions of narrative temporality. A great number of texts illustrating this operation have already been mentioned. Finally, rather than provide a list of examples, I prefer to focus on one story, perhaps more sophisticated and complex in terms of representations of time—one that, it is no coincidence, also exacerbates the questions of erudition and the conflicts between subjectivity and political history: "The Garden of Forking Paths" from *Fictions*.

The text develops two stories that correspond to two distinct conceptions of time. The first plot, which serves as a coherent framework for the whole, is a spy story. During the First World War, a Chinese man in London, working for the German intelligence service, has to pass secret information on to his superiors. This information concerns the location of the British artillery park in northern France, near the town of Albert. In order to communicate the name of the town, Yu Tsun decides to assassinate a man by the same name. According to his plans, the story is published in the newspapers and would then be known on the other side of the battlefront. Obviously, this task requires a variation on the motive for the crime, specific to detective novels (here, killing someone in order to make secret information known, without any connection to the victim). Yu Tsun identifies someone named Albert, living in the county of Staffordshire, goes to his house, kills him, and is arrested by the police for British counterespionage. The text that we are reading is an excerpt from a kind of confession written by the German spy on the eve of his execution.

The second plot, which is foreshadowed at the beginning of the story, focuses on one of Yu Tsun's ancestors, the writer and sage Ts'ui Pen. Stephen Albert, the man who was assassinated, is a specialist on his work and manages to unravel the mystery of the great work Ts'ui Pen wrote just before also being assassinated, a novel that would remain unexplained, *The Garden of Forking Paths*. For an hour, Albert explains to Yu Tsun how the book works. It is both an enormous riddle whose solution is "time" and a labyrinth (a "labyrinth of symbols," "an invisible labyrinth of time"[6]).

This improbable book is built around the proliferation of storylines and incessant bifurcation, which do not take place in space, as in a traditional labyrinth, but in time. Each event is not followed by a single consequence, but by all the potential consequences that correspond to different series within time. Albert illustrates the operation with an example: "Fang, let's say, has a secret; a stranger knocks at his door; Fang decides to kill him. Naturally, there are various possible outcomes—Fang can kill the intruder, the intruder can kill Fang, they can both live, they can both be killed, and so on.

In Ts'ui Pen's novel, *all* the outcomes in fact occur; each is the starting point for further bifurcations."[7] Through its conception of time and the example given to explain it, this second story, in its own way, encompasses the first (especially the part where a stranger knocks at Albert's door and kills him), which becomes a possibility among an extensive range of possibilities.

What precedes is but a gross simplification of the argument of a text overdetermined by representations of time, with the multiple allusions and multiple conflicts that accompany them. But it might suffice to show the simultaneous presence of several different visions. Yet the story does include references to chronological time (the inevitable form of time): throughout the story Yu Tsun is counting hours and minutes, whether it be while completing his task or awaiting his imminent death. At the same time, another series of elements indicates the presence of circular time: Albert's death is a repetition of Ts'ui Pen's death and even of his character Fang's death. But, of course, the most spectacular part of the story remains the idea of bifurcating time.

An essay included in *Other Inquisitions*, "Time and J. W. Dunne," introduces the erudite counterpoint to such a vision. Although Leibnitz's monads or possible worlds are not far from "The Garden," the direct source of inspiration seems to be Borges's reading of a book by Dunne, *Nothing Dies*, a book that imagines "an infinite number of times" that include the future, which already exists, and times that are conceived of as part of a fourth dimension of space.[8] He finds a justification for this idea in his premonitory dreams: "Dunne, surprisingly, supposes that eternity is already ours and that the dreams we have each night corroborate this. According to him, the immediate past and the immediate future flow together in our dreams." To explain this theory, he cites Schopenhauer when he wrote that "life and dreams were pages from the same book, and that to read them in their proper order was to live, but to scan them at random was to dream." Although Borges remains skeptical of these ideas, Dunne's conclusion amazes him: "Dunne assures us that in death we shall learn how to handle eternity successfully. We shall recover all the moments of our lives and we shall combine them as we please. God and our friends and Shakespeare will collaborate with us" (21). Temporal proliferation is a dream that cancels out the inevitable loss involved in every decision or action; hope and forgetting, like literature, can change the content of the times.

For Borges, the plasticity of time—just as much as erudition or the biographical pattern—is a catalyst for fiction, a production machine, a means to destabilize certainties and beliefs, in keeping with fantasy literature, but it is also the expression, both melancholic and appeasing, of a very personal obsession. Nonetheless, beyond its functional, erudite, or subjective facets, this systematic practice of questioning linear conceptions of time has immense consequences for the representation of history, be it social or literary. Here, as a conclusion to this presentation of the figure and of the work of Borges, are a few ideas and a few specific examples that concern these two notions.

Literary History: Novelty and Anachronism

At the crossroad of philosophical fabulations on time and inventions resulting from the careless practice of erudition, Borges developed a unique thought system on the historicity of texts, on the function of precursors in literature, on originality and rupture, and finally, on the connections of works to the time periods of their production. His influence over the habitual conceptions of historicity and over the ways of apprehending an alternative literary history has been immense. In "Pierre Menard," as we remember, it was already a matter of enriching the art of reading by way of "new techniques": "deliberate anachronism" and "fallacious attribution," according to the narrator of the story. The author from Nîmes was wary of the "elementary notion that all times and places are the same, or are different."[9] The erudite proliferation at work here has already been commented on; let us now turn to the question of anachronism and, therefore, of the temporality of texts—their succession in a chronological line and their relationship to a time period or to a context of production.

Borges exposes his disbelief before the supposed determinisms of specific time periods, whatever they may be, over writing. On many occasions, he remarked that every writer's belonging to his time period is unavoidable, without that implying the existence of textual traits that might represent it. The reasoning resembles what he says about being Argentine: being in one's time is either inevitable or a sham. In 1969, on the occasion of the republishing of *Luna de enfrente*, he stated, in contradiction with the avant-garde tone and with the goal of innovating put forth in this book of his youth, "To be modern is to be contemporary, of our own time; inevitably, we must be so."[10] Belonging to a time period is hence an irrelevant fact, in that it explains nothing. For this reason, he believes that real intellectuals must flee contemporary debates, for reality is "always anachronous";[11] furthermore, in his interviews, he often cites an aphorism of Flaubert's: "When a line is good, it loses its belonging to a school."[12] The writer's necessary and maybe even beneficial wariness toward schools of thought and current literary events is a constant. It is part of the autobiographical story studied here, through which he distances himself from his radical youth and reinforces the convictions of his mature years. But his wariness is also due to a more general stance taken on the questions of originality, progress, and rewriting, all of which are understood as part of historical development.

Let us look at a poem that illustrates this, "Ars Poetica," which addresses with a sobriety that no one could call classic the questions of novelty and of the intemporal essence of literature. This is a late text (prepublication in 1958) whose programmatic tone is foreshadowed in the title. The links between writing and temporality are set out from the very first stanza:

> To look at the river made of time and water
> And remember that time is another river.
> To know that we are lost like the river
> And that faces dissolve like water.[13]

Writing corresponds to actions that are listed here: going from "seeing" to "remembering" to "knowing"—perceiving a concrete reality (the river), associating it with the history of thought (through the reference to Heraclitus), with a traditional metaphor (life as a river), and with a melancholic sentiment (the inevitability of fleeting time).

Straight away, Borges deals with the known or even conventional aspects of the relationship of man to time to then update the common clichés surrounding poetic writing. This decision to repeat and to be unoriginal is reinforced by the rhymes that are but a basic repetition or the same word (water/water, river/river). Obviously, to the extent that original metaphors, surprising rhymes, and the refusal to rhyme have long been advocated by the poetic avant-garde, these choices are provocative if you will, but in a sense unexpected: the classical forms, the "eternal" subjects, the rhetoric coded by tradition appear as a kind of writing program and, in the end, as an peculiar form of originality.

The next part of the poem builds on the elements of the first part. Other conventional metaphors are introduced (death/sleep, sunset/old age, mirrors/art) with emphasis on the cyclical returning of the elements that make up poetry. As a conclusion, the two final stanzas move more toward an explicit definition of the essence of art. Borges offers up a kind of allegory of art and of its relationship to newness by turning to a reference of great cultural legitimacy, Ulysses:

> They say that Ulysses, sated with marvels,
> Wept tears of love at the sight of his Ithaca,
> Green and humble. Art is that Ithaca
> Of green eternity, not of marvels.

Writing is therefore posited as a kind of return to its legendary sources (*The Odyssey*), in search of modesty that might bring with it eternity, to the contrary of the ephemeral prodigy of trends and of the avant-garde.

The last stanza insists on the transhistoricity of poetry, not only in what it says but also in the way it is said through a form of rewriting that is emphasized:

> It [art] is also like the river with no end
> That flows and remains and is the mirror of one same
> Inconstant Heraclitus, who is the same
> And is another, like the river with no end.

This masterful stanza indicates a circular movement (art is also the river that runs and stays and it is also Heraclitus, inconstant, for it is, like the river, unending), a phenomenon that we can only consider original: art, whose essence seems to be time, is the same and it is other; it repeats itself, transforms and innovates through materials found in the lands of classics.

In "Ars Poetica," we find a conception of the temporality of art opposed to any radical evolution, to rupture, and to any form of amnesia; it is, on the contrary, the itinerary through the literary past that allows us to approach the unknown. Art is both circular (everything repeats itself, the materials are the same) and linear (reuse transforms and projects personal writing toward a renewed form of originality). Borges changes his strategy but not his objective: he is still aiming to propose a singular artistic creation. In that regard, the oxymoron is again a consistent main source; it is the literary form of his aesthetic vision. The ideal of superior art and the ideal of perfection continue to be present, even if it is no longer a matter of innovation nor of change, even if he is not associated with an aesthetic revolution, which he considers unachievable. For Borges, the future—the desired work—is not what will be written, but that which leaves traces to be followed in the books of the past.

Literary History: Inventing One's Precursors

Besides the paradox of newness built around repetition, and consequently, the hypothesis of the stability of forms, another remarkable aspect of this vision of the historicity of literature concerns the hierarchies of past/present and precursor/disciple. In "Kafka and His Precursors," Borges develops an idea on the question that is not entirely his own (should we be surprised?) as it had already been sketched out by T. S. Eliot and by Macedonio Fernández; nonetheless, his formulation has become a kind of legend. In reviewing "Kafka's precursors," Borges identifies the texts that present similarities to certain aspects of the Prague writer despite the great differences they possess: Zeno's paradox of Achilles and the turtle, a ninth century Chinese apologue, the works of Kierkegaard, a poem by Browning published in

1876, two stories by Léon Bloy. This series exists only because Kafka, arriving after all these texts, wrote a body of work that, in one way or another, resembles them. His work "noticeably refines and diverts" the readings that we might have of these authors; thus, the term *precursor* is cleansed of any controversial connotation or suggestion of rivalry: "The fact is that each writer *creates* his precursors. His work modifies our conception of the past, as it will modify the future."[14] To this extent, every work—and therefore every effect—transforms the past, that is to say, it chooses its origins. Literary history and the library are dynamic, evolutive spaces in which to discover new paths, suggest resemblances, and compare tones and ideas.

Moreover, it must be noted that the backward historicity hypothesized by Borges—the present that changes the past—offers a new conception of the precursor: a conception opposed both to the idea of the founder or the authority held by him, and to that which underlies the postmodern quote, seen as a means to recover material emptied of all value. In Borges's case, the relationship to a precursor established through posterity is that of an engendering: literary history is comprised of the reworking a few creations and a few names, each new work not being a mere imitation but, on the contrary, offering an increase in potential meaning. Kafka can therefore recover and enhance his precursors.[15] Such an upset in the order of generations and in the chronology of works, just as much as of the notion of originality and plagiarism, destabilizes many conceptions on which academic traditions are anchored. He was able to justify or inspire confrontational theories, like that of Pierre Bayard in his book *Le Plagiat par anticipation* (2009; Plagiarism by anticipation), according to which Proust did not follow in the footsteps of Maupassant, but Maupassant plagiarized Proust, for example. Literary history has ceased to be seen as a linear succession of ways of reading that, at each stage, transform the previous ones. In "For Bernard Shaw," Borges expands on this conception to include the future: "One literature differs from another, either before or after it, not so much because of the text as for the manner in which it is read. If I were able to read any contemporary page—this one, for example—as it would be read in the year 2000, I would know what literature would be like in the year 2000."[16] The past is a form of present in that it is on the writing table when the writer begins to write. The long-lasting concept of influence therefore explodes from within and the historicity of the works is revisited in a radical way.

This upheaval of chronology opens alternative paths to locating the historicity of works, to the extent that they cease to belong to a single time period in history. Thus, anachronism is a form of writing, a means for situating oneself in time, and even the equivalent to the historicity of texts. Literature is seen as a practice of distorting time according to which a multitude of time periods overlap both at the time of reading and at the time of writing. What therefore characterizes the writer is precisely this being out of one's time in order to better belong to it, or to better understand its preoccupations. A similar hypothesis is developed by Giorgio Agamben in *Qu'est-ce que le contemporain?* (2008; What is the contemporary?).

Social History: Barbarity

What precedes is not far from another idea, or more precisely another recurrent reverie: that of imagining that the present can not only predict and therefore transform the future, but that it can also modify the past. This possibility and this desire to see an impossible fact materialize are often stated in a variety of ways, but with remarkable consistency. The ability to recover lost objects through memory in the world of Tlön provided invaluable services, for it made it "possible not only to interrogate but even to modify the past, which is now no less plastic, no less malleable than the future."[17] In "Note for a Fantastic Story," Borges anticipates one day discovering "the divine art of undoing time or, as Pietro Damiano said, of altering the past."[18] He salutes, in "On Oscar Wilde," the lucidity of the author who believed that "to repent of an action is to modify the past,"[19] and in "Another Poem of the Gifts," expresses gratitude for the gifts received, notably that of forgetfulness, "which annuls or modifies the past."[20]

The malleability of the past and the conventional nature of its representation, which authorizes alternative versions and subsequent modifications (as was the case for biography), explains the importance of the point that remains to be discussed, namely the conception of social history in Borges's work. This plasticity of time, as much as the skepticism toward established or sacralized truths, leads the author to consider the relativity of the fruits of "national narratives" and to create, through unique narrative predictions, dystopic, detrimental and oppressive worlds in which we can recognize the totalitarian systems of the twentieth century.

Despite the distance kept from any form of belonging to his time, one of the most important events impressing on the production context of Borges's main texts was, as we know, the Second World War and its aftermath; the three books at the heart of his lifework (*Fictions*, *The Aleph*, and *Other Inquisitions*) were written during this conflict and immediately following it. If the conceptions of literature they convey reject the chronology of works, it is at the same time quite evident that these texts enter into dialogue with this unique period of Western history. In addition, it should be noted that the consistent representation of totalitarianism and the examination of the narratives on human societies contradicts the habitual perception of Borges's work as a textual corpus having turned its back on social history, context, and politics.[21] It is true, however, that Borges was often politically involved, on a personal level—after 1955, this engagement would take on a sinister orientation with the support of several military dictatorships—though there is no textual counterpart to these positions. Yet this is not the case with regard to the 1939–1945 war, which is the event par excellence, the one that would allow him to develop a specific perception of history.

On this point, Borges appears to rework the nightmarish worlds of Kafka (or the famous words of Joyce on history, "a nightmare from which I am trying to awake," which Borges quotes in a prologue[22]), thus turning them into stories; his stories therefore offer us futuristic representations of despotic regimes. These organized and regulated worlds are those of Tlön and the Library of Babel, as well as of a Babylonian society (in "The Lottery in Babylon"[23]) in which a game (the lottery) progressively becomes the organizational rule of an oppressive and repressive society governed by a "Company" that dictates every event in human life through a random draw. These are stories that begin with a philosophical or mathematical hypothesis and end on a highly political note.

In this context, Borges often questions the fate of individuals—and of writers—before this consistent barbarism that takes control. In "The Secret Miracle,"[24] the protagonist, Jaromir Hladik, a Jewish writer living in Prague, is about to be shot by Nazis without having finished his play written in verse, *The Enemies*. He then asks God for one more year in order to finish this creation, and the extension is granted to him. At the precise moment when the squad is ready to shoot the decisive bullets, time stops, the soldiers and Hladik remain motionless, but Hladik can continue to think: he then writes, mentally, what was missing in order to complete his text. As soon as he finds the last word, fire rains down on him, and he is killed, as planned.

Stranger and even more ambiguous is the fable presented a few years later in *"Deutsches Requiem,"* in *The Aleph*, a story comprised of ten thoughts in the mind of a vice-director of a Nazi concentration camp who showed no pity toward a Jewish poet, David Jerusalem, notwithstanding his immense admiration for Jerusalem's poetry. The description of the character of the vice-director is troubling, as he appears to be an educated person (he cites Goethe, Nietzsche, Spengler, *De rerum natura*, the theologians, and Schopenhauer) and his atrocious destiny an utter coincidence. Nonetheless, at the end of the story, just before he faces death—he ends up being executed—he recalls the happiness that the defeat of Germany brought him. Not because of guilt or an awareness of the uselessness of having regrets, but because this defeat implies a step toward the triumph of "violence and faith in the sword."[25] The destruction of Germany is the price to pay in order to build a "new order," a new era that is, according to the vice-director, the great work of Nazism. German influence will always be present precisely through the mark of barbarism that it will have left on Europe.

This specular and disturbing representation (the narrator, a symbol of evil, is reminiscent of Borges and therefore of all men), this vision of what Borges called "the tragedy of the German fate,"[26] and this paradoxical overview of the war (seen not as the triumph of freedom, but as the triumph of warmongering and confrontation) was written, surprisingly, very early on, in 1946. Thus, the protagonist of the story, like all of Germany, was destined to die but foreshadows the future: "Tomorrow I shall die, but I am a symbol of the generations to come" is the narrator's frightening prediction.[27]

Social History: National Heroes

The meaning and functions of history are at the heart of these texts in which echoes of the Second World War resonate. On a completely different level, Borges often spoke of how his father, an anarchist, denounced a moralizing instrumentalization of history that edified or exemplified Argentine national history, especially in schools. Following the troubles that came after Independence and during the process of nation-building, a legendary version of the past indeed became dominant, a narrative that was both epic (by way of its exaltation of a few heroic figures whose personality was seen as exemplary) and harmonious; despite the bloody conflicts, the emphasis was on the result, the construction of a human community imagined to be exceptional. Before such a phenomenon, Jorge Borges believed—or at least that is what his son remembers—that national history had replaced catechism in Argentina.

This vision of history as a religion, in the sense of faith, proselytism, and the simplified narrative that it contains, is clear in many of Borges's texts that deconstruct the substructures of these types of beliefs. On the one hand, we find a certain nihilism tending toward discrediting the proof conveyed by these mythicized narratives, and on the other, a distrust of the spectacular and theatrical and of the equivocal assertion of meaning as altogether determined.

One of the short stories in *Fictions*, "The Theme of the Traitor and the Hero" (first published in 1944) faces these questions directly. The story focuses on the doubt raised over the true personality and actual actions of a national hero. The narrator playfully hesitates, at the beginning of his story, on the country in which he will situate the events of his story: "Poland, Ireland, the Republic of Venice, some South American or Balkan state . . ."[28] And in the end, he decides on Ireland during the wars of independence of the first third of the nineteenth century. Yet, this decision fools no one, as the iconography as well as the attributes of the hero, Fergus Kilpatrick, correspond astonishingly to those of Latin American figures: Bolívar, San Martín, Artigas. In addition, and according to the first portrait painted of Kilpatrick, he was not only the chief conspirator (a "secret and glorious captain of conspirators"), he was also the equivalent of Moses, "who from the land of Moab glimpsed yet could not reach the promised land"; likewise, "Kilpatrick perished on the eve of the victorious rebellion he had planned for and dreamed of" (143). The mythical analogy, we must admit, is not banal.

The story itself is built around an earlier investigation conducted by Ryan, a descendent of Kilpatrick, in 1924; the investigation underscores the variability of possible interpretations of the hero's life. This investigation, justified by the intention of writing a book on the matter, leads Ryan to discover some strange facts: Kilpatrick was killed in a theater by an assassin who was never identified. His last days and last hours mimicked those of Julius Cesar; and worse, they mimicked Shakespeare's version of the events (in *Julius Cesar*) and even included lines from other plays by the author (such as *Macbeth*). This strange coincidence allows, without any explanation as to exactly how, for an important secret to be revealed. At the end of the story, we find a detailed explanation that sets the facts straight, like in a detective novel.

According to this explanation, Kilpatrick, believing that the conspiracy he was part of had failed at every attempt, requested an investigation in order to reveal the traitor who was surely responsible for this turn of events. As it had happened to Oedipus, the investigation that he requested would lead to the undeniable conclusion that he himself, Kilpatrick, was the culprit. He is sentenced to death and signs by his own hand the sentence; but he did even more: he asked to die as a hero in order to contribute to the fight for Irish independence. One of his disciples then quickly writes a play-script that transforms the punishment of a traitor into the creation of an epic martyr. In order to do so as quickly as possible, he plagiarizes Shakespeare, the great literary figure of England, the land of the enemy. Kilpatrick's death was, literally, a play in which hundreds of actors and extras participated. Everything had been planned beforehand, even the few words he would utter just before dying, "between two spurts of sudden blood." Rather, everything was planned, but Kilpatrick sometimes diverged from the script through "improvised words and acts," the twists that would then justify his posthumous glory. He died "in a box (prefiguring Lincoln's) draped with funeral curtains," which suggests in passing the existence of other repetitions and other fictions.

Ryan discovers this paradoxical truth according to which the national hero of Ireland was in fact a traitor, or more precisely, both a traitor and a hero. For in betraying the conspirators, he attempted to prevent his country's independence, but he also faced death with extreme determination and courage in order to effectively create a heroic figure that would make this same independence possible. As we can observe, Borges does not turn to psychology to explain this behavior; there is instead a logical apparatus that allows for Kilpatrick, according to the facts presented, to exist as either traitor or hero—this variability was, as we know, often characteristic of Borges's biographies. The meaning of one's life is undetermined, or at least relative. His story, the national narrative, and the glorious struggle for the independence of his country are marked by, or even determined by, an artificial element inspired by the culture of the enemy (Shakespeare) to better defend this same independence. The idea is disturbing.

But is this merely a deconstruction of the mechanisms governing national narratives? By upsetting any clear and simple interpretation, Borges adds, in the second edition of the text, a final paragraph to the conclusion which, in the first version, was the story of Kilpatrick's assassination. In the new ending, the narrator specifies that Ryan, a century after the death of his ancestor, decided to hide his discovery and write, as planned, a book glorifying the hero on the occasion of the hundred-year commemoration of his death. After initially highlighting the uncertainty of meaning in biography and the artificial nature of national narratives, this conclusion introduces a third level of meaning: despite it all, despite the construction at work and its ambiguities, the national narrative is effective. Independence is won and consequently, the glory of the hero honored. This is perhaps the reason why this story must be preserved.[29]

The Inevitable

The question of time and the becoming of history appears, therefore, as a counterpoint to the unresolved issue of meaning, highly present elsewhere in the body of works. Though these literary fables introduce imaginative variations on a given invariable, that of the history of humankind, Borges positions himself in a clearly autonomous space, ridden of obligations that govern the historiographic narrative, far from a conception of time as collective, coded, intelligible, stable. This freedom allows him to explore the multiple facets of imaginary time: the unimagined or unimaginable dimensions of time materialize in different forms that, in that way, corroborate the literary story. Borrowing from Paul Ricoeur, we can say that temporal aporias become productive; they integrate a kind of remythification of time.[30]

Borges appears to be obsessed with transforming the past, with the inversion of generational order, and with the desire to be a protagonist in what has already occurred; he also wishes to get as close as possible to a form of eternity that might cancel out loss, or give it life through some form of possession. His domain is literary time, which differs from that of the calendar and with each reading emerges continuously renewed. Thus, he seeks to alter the causal chain by reversing the aphorism *post hoc, ergo propter hoc* (after this, therefore because of this) in order for the impossible to become possible. In its meandering, the course of invented time often becomes nightmarish or cosmic, but in any case, it remains malleable.

However, we mustn't overestimate this pervasive aspect of Borges's work that inscribes it in the tradition of fantasy literature, to the extent that these representations are not proposals on the universe, but reveries. In fact, some form of the inevitable is the basis for these variations. This is particularly true for the representation of historical time.

Time, according to Ts'ui Pen in *The Garden of Forking Paths*, can indeed vary its potentiality and multiply infinitely, but Albert will indeed be assassinated, Yu Tsun is about to be executed and the bombing of the English artillery park will take place. In "The Wall and the Books," there is a profound interrogation into the meaning of a historical event (the construction of the Great Wall of China and the destruction of the library by the same emperor), but, be that as it may, the wall was erected and the books were burned. The final outcomes of "Tlön, Uqbar, Orbis Tertius" point to the possibility of inventing a different world and time, which could be interpreted as an attempt to flee the horrors that history offered in 1940, and nonetheless, the destruction of the world will inevitably take place. In "The Theme of the Traitor and the Hero," despite the multiplicity of versions and their ambiguity, the independence of Ireland is a fact, and the role of its national heroes is undeniable. In "The Secret Miracle," even if the costliest of human dreams is played out (stopping time at a crucial moment), the result of the miracle is negligible; no one will read Hladik's work and he will be shot dead.

Borges's literature deploys various representations of transgressions, rantings, and temporal variations that, each step of the way, contradict, refute, and destabilize chronological time and offer, on the contrary, with vehement creativity, alternative conceptions of time. Yet, as occurs with all forms of opposition, this deploying extends and updates what is denied. Even though chronological time ceases to be an apparent and natural axis, even though it is turned into a construction among others, the mechanism breaks down when up against a wall with no visible cracks: the ignominy of death and of the horrors of history.

The mythical figure of destiny cannot intervene, in its own way, in these fictional stories; there must be something exterior, outside of literature, something indescribable, unattainable, but active—as the "real" is in psychoanalysis. Yes, literature, for Borges, offers the possibility of revising the course of history; it opens discussion on its "truths," but it cannot transform the consequences of history, that iron chain of events that was particularly tragic in the 1930s and 1940s. In literary time, variation displaces authority and reworks traditions, but with regard to history, the implacable law of chronology is always enforced, despite the ardors of human imagination. Borges's texts also tell of this ordinary drama.

Please allow me to end this presentation of the Argentine writer with an excerpt, in which the questions of the subject, time, melancholy, erudition, and other themes of his work are virtuously intertwined. It is the final paragraph of "A New Refutation of Time," which closes out a series of commentaries on different authors and thought systems that, in one way or another, question the conception of time as an inevitable succession:

> *And yet, and yet* ... To deny temporal succession, to deny the self, to deny the astronomical universe, appear to be acts of desperation and are secret consolations. Our destiny (unlike the hell of Swedenborg and the hell of Tibetan mythology) is not terrifying because it is unreal; it is terrifying because it is irreversible and iron-bound. Time is the substance of which I am made. Time is a river that sweeps me along, but I am the river; it is a tiger that mangles me, but I am the tiger; it is a fire that consumes me, but I am the fire. The world, unfortunately, is real; I, unfortunately, am Borges.[31]

NOTES

INTRODUCTION

1. Hannah Arendt, *Walter Benjamin* (Paris: Allia, 2007), 64.
2. Jorge Luis Borges, "Sobre los clásicos," [On the classics] in *Obras completas II* [Complete works in Spanish II] (Buenos Aires: Emecé, 2007), 184–85. Translator's note: This and all translations of texts in French and Spanish without published translations are the translator's. I thank Nicolás Lucero for his judicious aid in locating existing translations of Borges's works. Readers should also note that most of the discussions in this book focus on the original Spanish versions of Borges's works, but quotes and references are provided in English to facilitate readers' understanding.
3. Daniel Balderston, *Out of Context: Historical Reference and the Representation of Reality in Borges* (Durham, NC: Duke University Press, 1993).
4. Gérard Genette, *Narrative Discourse*, trans. Jane E. Lewin (Ithaca, NY: Cornell University Press, 1980), 30.

PART I

1. Jorge Luis Borges, "Poem of Gifts," trans. Alastair Reid, in *Selected Poems*, ed. Alexander Coleman, (London: Penguin, 1999), 97.
2. Jorge Luis Borges, "Profesión de fe literaria," [Literary profession of faith] in *El tamaño de mi esperanza* [The full extent of my hope] (Barcelona: Seix Barral, 1994), 128.

CHAPTER 1

1. Borges, "The Full Extent of My Hope," trans. Alfred Mac Adam, in *On Argentina*, ed. Alfred Mac Adam and Suzanne Jill Levine (New York: Penguin, 2010), 48.
2. Ibid., 47.
3. Ibid., 79.
4. Borges, "The Streets," trans. Stephen Kessler, in *Selected Poems*, 5.
5. Borges, "Unknown Street," trans. Alexander Coleman, in *Selected Poems*, 11.
6. Borges, "Patio," trans. R. F. in *Selected Poems*, 15.
7. Borges, "The South," trans. W. S. Merwin, in *Selected Poems*, 9.
8. Borges, "Arrabal," [Outskirts] in *Obras completas I* [Complete works in Spanish I] (Buenos Aires: Emecé, 2007), 35.
9. Borges, "The Full Extent," 47.
10. Adolfo Bioy Casares, *Borges* (Buenos Aires: Destino, 2006), 120.
11. Readers should note that the terms relating to "suburbia" (*suburbio*) in the context of Argentina do not denote what they do in the context of the United States. The suburbs in Argentina, as in Europe, are the less nice areas of a city.
12. Borges, "Barrio reconquistado" [Neighborhood reconquered], in *Obras completas I*, 129.
13. Borges, "The Full Extent," 46.
14. Jorge Luis Borges, *Textos recobrados 1919–1929* [Recovered texts 1919–1929] (Buenos Aires: Emecé, 1997), 101.
15. Jorge Luis Borges, *Œuvres complètes I* [Complete works in French] (Paris: Gallimard, Bibliothèque de la Pléiade, 1993), ix.
16. Borges, "The Pampa and the *Suburbio* Are Gods," trans. Alfred Mac Adam, in *On Argentina*, 49–52.
17. Borges, *Textos recobrados*, 101.
18. Ibid., 104.
19. Borges, "The Mythical Founding of Buenos Aires," trans. Alistair Reid, in *Selected Poems*, 53.
20. Ibid., 55
21. Ibid.
22. Jorge Luis Borges, "Valéry as a Symbol," in *Other Inquisitions: 1937–1952*, trans. Ruth L. C. Simms (Austin: University of Texas Press, 1964), 73.
23. Pezzoni, Enrique. "*Fervor de Buenos Aires*: Autobiografía y autorretrato." [Fervor of Buenos Aires: Autobiography and self-portrait] In *El texto y sus voces* [The text and its voices]. Buenos Aires: Sudamericana, 1986, 76.
24. Jorge Luis Borges, *El idioma de los Argentinos* [The language of the Argentines] (Madrid: Alianza, 1998), 98.
25. Borges, "La vuelta" [The return], in *Obras completas I*, 20.
26. Borges, "Arrabal" [The outskirts], in *Obras completas I*, 35.
27. Jorge Luis Borges, "An Autobiographical Essay," in *The Aleph and Other Stories: 1933–1969* (New York: E.P. Dutton, 1970), 221–22.
28. Jorge Luis Borges, "Ultraísmo," *Nosotros* (Buenos Aires) 39, no. 151 (December 1921): 466–71.
29. Jorge Luis Borges, *Inquisiciones* (Barcelona: Seix Barral, 1994), 31.
30. Jorge Luis Borges, "La simulación

de la imagen," [The simulation of the image] in *El idioma de los Argentinos*, 82–83.
31. Borges, "Campos atardecidos" [Fields at twilight], in *Obras completas I*, 55.
32. Borges, "Gesta maximalista" [Maximal achievement] in *Textos recobrados*, 89.
33. Borges, *El tamaño*, 43.
34. Borges, "Examen de metáforas," [Examination of metaphors] in *Inquisiciones*, 72.
35. Jorge Luis Borges, "Pascal's Sphere," in *Selected Non-fictions*, ed. Eliot Weinberger, trans. Esther Allen, Suzanne Jill Levine, and Eliot Weinberger (New York: Penguin, 1999), 351.
36. Borges, "Nathaniel Hawthorne," in *Other Inquisitions*, 47.
37. Alan Pauls, *Le Facteur Borges* [The Borges factor] (Paris: Christian Bourgois, 2006), 20–52.
38. Borges, "Leopold Lugones: *Romancero*," in *On Argentina*, 57.
39. Borges, *El tamaño*, 107–9.
40. Borges, *El idioma*, 92.
41. Borges, "Ejecución de tres palabras," in *Inquisiciones*, 163.
42. Jorge Luis Borges, "Tlön, Uqbar, Orbis Tertius," in *Collected Fictions*, trans. Andrew Hurley (New York: Penguin, 1998), 77.
43. Borges, "An Autobiographical Essay," in *The Aleph*, 225.
44. Ibid., 228.
45. Ibid., 225.
46. Borges, "The Nothingness of Personality," trans. Esther Allen, in *Selected Non-fictions*, 3–9.
47. Borges, "An Autobiographical Essay," 231.
48. Ibid.
49. Pauls, *Le facteur Borges*, 20–24.
50. Michel Lafon, *Borges, ou, La réécriture* [Borges, or, Rewriting] (Paris: Seuil, 1990), 81.
51. Ricardo Piglia, "Ideología y ficción en Borges" [Ideology and fiction in Borges], in *Ficciones Argentinas: Antología de lecuras críticas* [Argentine fictions: Anthology of critical readings], ed. Argentine Literature Research Group of the UBA (Buenos Aires: Norma, 2004), 33–42.
52. Borges, "The Full Extent," 47–48.
53. Ibid., 48.
54. Borges, "Averroës' Search," in *Collected Fictions*, 235–241.
55. Lafon, *Borges, ou, La réécriture*, 90.
56. Borges, "Prologue," in *Selected Poems*, 35.
57. Borges, *Obras completas I*, 61.
58. Ibid.
59. Ibid.
60. Ibid., 15.

CHAPTER 2

1. Borges, "Story of the Warrior and the Captive Maiden," in *Collected Fictions*, 208–11.
2. Borges, "Forward to Artifices," in *Collected Fictions*, 129.
3. Borges, "The South," in *Collected Fictions*, 174–179.
4. Didier Anzieu, "Le corps et le code dans les contes de Borges" [The body and the code in Borges's short

stories], in *Le Corps de l'œuvre* [The body of the work] (Paris: Gallimard, 1981), 300.
5. Emir Rodríguez Monegal, *Borges: Hacia una interpretación* [Borges: Toward an interpretation] (Madrid: Guadarrama, 1976), 92.
6. Borges, "An Autobiographical Essay," in *The Aleph*, 211.
7. Ibid., 241.
8. Jean de Milleret and Dominique Roux, ed. *Entretiens* [Interviews] (Paris: Cahier de l'Herne, 1981), 70–71.
9. Borges, "An Autobiographical Essay," in *The Aleph*, 242.
10. Jorge Luis Borges, "Pierre Menard, Author of the Quixote," in *Collected Fictions*, 88–95.
11. Lafon, *Borges, ou, La réécriture*, 103.
12. Rodríguez Monegal, *Borges*, 92.
13. Borges, "Hombres pelearon," [Men fought] in *El idioma*, 133–35.
14. Borges, "An Autobiographical Essay," in *The Aleph*, 237.
15. Ibid.
16. *Historia universal de la infamia* was published in English translation twice, as *A Universal History of Infamy* in 1972 (trans. Norman Thomas di Giovanni), and as *A Universal History of Iniquity* in 2004 (trans. Andrew Hurley).
17. Borges, "The Dead Man," in *Collected Fictions*, 196.
18. Borges, "An Autobiographical Essay," in *The Aleph*, 237.
19. Ibid.
20. Borges, "Preface to the First Edition," in *Collected Fictions*, 3.
21. Borges, "Autobiographical Essay," in *The Aleph*, 238.
22. Ibid., 239.
23. Rodríguez Monegal, *Borges*, 200.
24. Borges, "El pasado" [The past], in *Obras completas II*, 533.
25. Borges, "Pierre Menard," in *Collected Fictions*, 91.
26. Enrique Pezzoni, *Enrique Pezzoni, lector de Borges* [Enrique Pezzoni, reader of Borges], ed. Annick Louis, ed. (Buenos Aires: Sudamerica, 1999), 49.
27. Michel Foucault, *The Order of Things: An Archaeology of the Human Sciences* (New York: Taylor & Francis, 2005), 16.
28. Pauls, *Le Facteur Borges*, 126.
29. Borges, "Tlön, Uqbar," in *Collected Fictions*, 79–81.
30. Borges, "The Mythical Founding of Buenos Aires," in *Selected Poems*, 53–55.
31. Gerard Genette, "Utopie Littéraire," in *Figures I* (Paris: Seuil, 1966), 130; trans. Marcy Schwartz, from her unpublished translation.
32. Didier Anzieu, forward to *Le Secret de Borges* [The secret of Borges], by Julio Woscoboinik (Lyon: Césura Lyon, 1989), 9–10.
33. Woscoboinik, *Le Secret de Borges*, 9–10.
34. Borges, "For Bernard Shaw," *Other Inquisitions*, 164.
35. Borges, "Tlön, Uqbar," in *Collected Fictions*, 74.
36. Borges, "A New Refutation of Time," trans. Suzanne Jill Levine, in *Selected Non-fictions*, 317.
37. Borges, "The House of Asterion," in *Collected Fictions*, 221.
38. Borges, "The Total Library," in *Selected Non-fictions*, 216.

39. Borges, "The Library of Babel," in *Collected Fictions*, 115.
40. Borges, *Œuvres complètes I*, 1581–82.
41. Anzieu, "Le Corps et le code," 307.
42. Borges, "The Total Library," in *Selected Non-fictions*, 216.
43. Jean Starobinski, "La mélancolie de l'anatomiste," *Tel Quel*, no.10 (1962): 21–29.
44. Borges, "The Library of Babel," in *Collected Fictions*, 112.
45. Ibid.
46. Starobinski, "La mélancolie," 26.
47. Borges, *Selected Non-fictions*, 341–43.
48. Giorgio Agamben, *Stanzas: Word and Phantasms in Western Culture*, trans. Ronald L. Martinez (Minneapolis: University of Minnesota Press, 1993), 19–21.
49. Borges, "A New Refutation of Time," in *Selected Non-fictions*, 323.
50. Borges, "1964," trans. Alistair Reid, in *Selected Poems*, 217.
51. Yves Bonnefoy, preface to *La Melancolie au miroir: Trois lectures de Baudelaire* [Melancholy in the mirror: Three readings of Baudelaire], by Jean Starobinski (Paris: Julliard, 1989), 8.
52. Borges, "The Library of Babel," in *Collected Fictions*, 112.
53. Sigmund Freud, "Mourning and Melancholia," (1917) trans. Joan Rivière, in *Collected Papers*, vol. IV, (London: Hogarth Press, 1950), 152–70.
54. Borges, "Poem of the Gifts," trans. Alistair Reid, in *Selected Poems*, 95.

CHAPTER 3

1. Borges, "Isidoro Acevedo," *Obras completas I*, 96.
2. Martin S. Stabb, "Introduction: Borges and His Critics." In *Jorge Luis Borges: An Annotated Primary and Secondary Bibliography*, by David William Foster (New York: Garland, 1984).
3. De Man, Paul. "A Modern Master." *New York Review of Books*, March, 9, 1964.
4. John Updike, "The Author as a Librarian," *New Yorker*, October 30, 1965; John Barth, "The Literature of Exhaustion," *Atlantic*, August 1967, 29–34.
5. Borges, *An Autobiographical Essay*, 249–50.
6. Ibid.
7. Borges, "An Autobiographical Essay," 252.
8. Borges, "Afterword," in *Collected Fictions*, 327.
9. Borges, "Borges and I," in *Collected Fictions*, 324.
10. Ibid.
11. Michel Foucault, "What Is an Author?" (1969), in *Modernity and its Discontents*, ed. James L. Marsh, John D. Caputo, and Merold Westphal (New York: Fordham University Press, 1992), 307.
12. Borges, "Forward to *Brodie's Report*," in *Collected Fictions*, 346.
13. Borges, "Poem of the Gifts," 95.
14. Borges, "In Praise of Darkness," trans. Hoyt Rogers, in *Selected Poems*, 299–301.

15. Gayle Talese, "Argentine Here on Lecture Tour Finds Advantages in Blindness," *New York Times*, February 5, 1962.
16. Borges, "Forward: For Leopoldo Lugones," in *Collected Fictions*, 291.
17. Borges, "The Maker," in *Collected Fictions*, 292–93.
18. Borges, "Everything and Nothing," in *Collected Fiction*, 320.
19. Borges, "Tlön, Uqbar," in *Collected Fictions*, 76.
20. Borges, "Afterword to the Maker," in *Collected Fictions*, 327.
21. Borges, "Prologue to *The Self and the Other*," in *Selected Poems*, 149.
22. Borges, "The Other," in *Collected Fictions*, 416.
23. Borges, "August 25, 1983," in *Collected Fictions*, 493.
24. Ibid., 490.
25. Borges, "Shakespeare's Memory," in *Collected Fictions*, 508.
26. Ibid., 514.
27. Borges, "Prologue," in *Selected Poems*, 371.
28. Borges, "Abramowicz," *Obras completas III*, 558.
29. Borges, "Someone," in *Selected Poems*, 225.
30. Borges, "You are Not the Others," in *Selected Poems*, 385
31. Borges, "Milonga de Juan Muraña," in *Obras completas III*, 374.
32. Borges, "La Jonction," in *Atlas*, trans. Anthony Kerrigan (New York: E.P. Dutton, 1985), 73–74.
33. Borges, "Laprida," in *Atlas*, 77–81.
34. Borges, "Epilogue," in *Selected Poems*, 439.
35. Borges, "The Enigmas," in *Selected Poems*, 215.
36. Borges, "Eclesiastés I, 9," in *Obras completas III*, 358.
37. Borges, "Street Corners," in *Atlas*, 57.
38. Borges, "Yesterdays," in *Selected Poems*, 445.
39. Octave Mannoni, "Je sais bien, mais quand même" [I know well, but all the same], in *Clefs pour l'imaginaire, ou, L'autre scène* (Paris: Seuil, 1969), 9.
40. Borges, "Metaphors of the 1001 Nights," trans. Jack Ross, in *Historia de la noche* (1977), in *Magazine* 1 (2003), 36–38.
41. Borges, "The Immortal," in *Collected Fictions*, 194.

PART II

1. Borges, Jorge Luis, "Almost a Last Judgment," trans. Stephen Kessler, in *Poems of the Night*, Penguin Books, London, 1925, p. 33.
2. Italo Calvino, *Six Memos for the Next Millennium*, (Cambridge, MA: Harvard University Press, 1988), 51.
3. Michel Lafon, "Histoires infâmes, biographies synthétiques, fictions: Vies de Jorge Luis Borges," [Iniquitous stories, synthetic biographies, fictions: Lives of Jorge Luis Borges] in *Fictions biographiques: xixe–xxie siècles* [Biographical fictions: 19th–21st centuries], ed. Anne-Marie Monluçon and Agathe Salha, (Toulouse: Presses Universitaires du Mirail, 2007), 191–202.

CHAPTER 4

1. Borges, "Biography of Oscar Wilde," in *Textos cautivos: Ensayos y reseñas en 'El Hogar' (1936–1939)* [Captive texts: Essays and reviews in *El Hogar*] (Barcelona: Tusquets, 1986).
2. Bourdieu, Pierre "L'Illusion biographique" [The biographical illusion]. In *Raisons pratiques: Sur la théorie de l'action* (Paris: Seuil, 1994).
3. Borges, "The South," in *Collected Fictions*, 174.
4. Borges, "The Argentine Writer and Traditions," in *On Argentina*, 138.
5. Piglia, "Ideología y ficción en Borges," 34.
6. Borges, *Textos cautivos*, 162.
7. Michel Lafon, "Le foyer des fictions," in *Jorge Luis Borges: Les Essais*, Co-textes 38 (Montpellier: Institut de Sociocritique de Montpellier, 2001).
8. Borges, "A Life of Evaristo Carriego," in *Evaristo Carriego: A Book about Old-Time Buenos Aires*, trans. Norman Thomas Di Giovanni (New York: Dutton, 1984), 51.
9. Borges, "Forward to an Edition of the Complete Poems of Evaristo Carriego," in *Evaristo Carriego*, 129–30.
10. Borges, "A Biography of Tadeo Isidoro Cruz (1829–1874), in *Selected Poems*, 213.
11. Borges, "Conjectural Poem," trans. Alistair Reid, in *Selected Poems*, 159–161.
12. Borges, "An Autobiographical Essay," 238.
13. Marcel Schwob, preface to *Imaginary Lives*, trans. Chris Clarke (Cambridge, MA: Wakefield Press, 2018) 10.
14. Borges, "On William Beckford's Vathek," in *Selected Non-fictions*, 236.
15. Alexandre Gefen, "Dieu supposé (sur les *Vies imaginaires*)" [God imagined (on the *Imaginary lives*], in *Marcel Schwob d'hier et d'aujourd'hui* [Marcel Schwob today and yesterday], eds. Christian Berg and Yves Vadé, 194–220 (Seyssel: Champ Vallon, 2002).
16. Daniel Madelénat, *La Biographie* (Paris: PUF, 1984).
17. Borges, "The Cruel Redeemer Lazarus Morell," in *Collected Fictions*, 12.
18. Borges, "Funes, His Memory," in *Collected Fictions*, 131.
19. Borges, "The Story of the Warrior and the Captive," in *Collected Fictions*, 210.
20. Borges, *Textos recobrados*, 93.
21. Borges, "Coleridge's Flower," in *Selected Non-fictions*, 240.
22. Borges, "Narrative Art and Magic," in *Selected Non-fictions*, 82.
23. Ibid., 80–81.

CHAPTER 5

1. Borges, *Textos recobrados*, 353.
2. Borges, "Ibn-Hakam al-Bokhari, Murdered in His Labyrinth," in *Collected Fictions*, 256.
3. Borges, "The Mirror of the Enigmas," in *Other Inquisitions*, 128.
4. Borges, "Ibn-Hakam al-Bokhari," in *Collected Fictions*, 262.

5. Borges, "The Detective Story," in *Selected Non-fictions*, 492.
6. Parodi, Cristina. "Borges y la subversión del modelo policial," [Borges and the subversion of the model of the detective novel] in *Borges: Desesperaciones aparentes y consuelos secretos* [Borges: Feigned desperation and secret consolation], ed. Rafael Olea Franco. (Mexico: El Colegio de México, 1999), 77–97.
7. Borges, "The Library of Babel," 118.
8. Borges, "The Wall and the Books," in *Selected Non-fictions*, 344.
9. Borges, "The Mirror of the Enigmas," in *Other Inquisitions*, 128.
10. María Esther Vásquez, *Borges: Imágenes, memorias, diálogos* [Borges: Images, memories, dialogues] (Caracas: Monte Avila, 1977), 47.
11. Borges, "Nathaniel Hawthorne," 48.
12. Ibid., 62.
13. Borges, "For Bernard Shaw," in *Other Inquisitions*, 164.

CHAPTER 6

1. Borges, "Funes, His Memory," in *Collected Fictions*, 135.
2. Borges, "The Enigma of Edward FitzGerald," in *Selected Non-fictions*, 367.
3. Borges, "The Zahir," in *Collected Fictions*, 243.
4. Ricardo Piglia, *Crítica y ficción* (Buenos Aires: Siglo XX, 1990), 147.
5. "Epilogue," *Other Inquisitions*, p. 189.
6. Adolfo Bioy Casares, "*El jardín de los senderos que se bifurcan*." [The garden of forking paths], in *Jorge Luis Borges*, edited by Jaime Alazraki (Madrid: Taurus, [1942] 1976), 56.
7. Calvino, *Six memos*, 50.
8. Ibid., 50–51.
9. Borges, "Literary Pleasure," in *Selected Non-fictions*, 29.
10. Borges, "Prologue," in *Collected Fictions*, 66.
11. Borges, "Ragnarök," in *Collected Fictions*, 321.
12. Ibid., 322.
13. Sylvia Molloy, *Las letras de Borges* [The letters of Borges] (Buenos Aires: Sudamericana, 1979), 188.
14. Borges, "To a Minor Poet of the Greek Anthology," trans. W. S. Merwin, in *Selected Poems*, 167; "To a Minor Poet of 1899," trans. Charles Tomlinson, in *Selected Poems*, 205.
15. Borges, "The Argentine Writer and Tradition," *Selected Non-fictions*, 423–24.
16. Borges, "The Plot," in *Collected Fictions*, 307.
17. Borges, "The Gospel According to Mark," in *Collected Fictions*, 397–401.
18. Borges, "An Autobiographical Essay," 214.
19. Borges, "The Full Extent," 7–48.

CHAPTER 7

1. Borges, "A History of Eternity," in *Selected Non-fictions*, 123.
2. Paul Ricoeur, *Time and Narrative*, vol. 1, trans. Kathleen McLaughlin

and David Pellauer (Chicago: University of Chicago Press, 1990), 6.
3. Paul Ricoeur, "Fiction and Its Imaginative Variations on Time," in *Time and Narrative*, vol. 3, trans. Kathleen McLaughlin and David Pellauer, 127–42 (Chicago: University of Chicago Press, 2010).
4. Borges, "A History of Eternity," 138.
5. Ibid., 137–39.
6. Borges, "The Garden of Forking Paths," in *Collected Fictions*, 124.
7. Ibid., 125.
8. Borges, "Time and J. W. Dunne," in *Other Inquisitions*, 18.
9. Borges, "Pierre Menard," in *Collected Fictions*, 91.
10. Borges, "Prologue," in *Selected Poems*, 35.
11. Borges, "Two books," in *Selected Non-Fiction*, 209.
12. Gustave Flaubert, "Lettre à Louise Colet, June 25–26, 1853," in *Correspondance de Flaubert*, vol. 3 (Paris: Édition Conard, 1927), 249.
13. Borges, "Ars Poetica," in *Selected Poems*, 137.
14. Borges, "Kafka and His Precursors," in *Selected Non-fictions*, 363–365. Emphasis in original.
15. Judith Schlanger, "Le précurseur," [The precursor] in *Le temps des œuvres: Mémoire et préfiguration* [The time of works: Memory and foreshadowing], ed. Jacques Neefs (Saint-Denis: Presses Universitaires de Vincennes, 2001), 13–27.
16. Borges, "For Bernard Shaw," in *Other Inquisitions*, 164.
17. Borges, "Tlön, Uqbar," in *Collected Fictions*, 77–78.
18. Borges, "Note for a Fantastic Story," in *Selected Poems*, 437.
19. Borges, "On Oscar Wilde," in *Selected Non-fictions*, 315.
20. Borges, "Another Poem of the Gifts," trans. Alan Dugan, *Selected Poems 1923–67* (London: Penguin, 1989).
21. Balderston, *Out of Context*.
22. Borges, "Prólogo a *Facundo* de Domingo Faustino Sarmiento," [Prologue to *Facundo* by Domingo Faustino Sarmiento] in *Obras completas IV* (Buenos Aires: Emecé, 2007), 149–55.
23. Borges, "The Lottery in Babylon," in *Collected Fictions*, 101–6.
24. Borges, "The Secret Miracle," in *Collected Fictions*, 157–62.
25. Borges, "*Deutsches Requiem*," in *Collected Fictions*, 234.
26. James East Irby, *Encuentro con Borges* [Encounter with Borges] (Mexico City: Universidad de Mexico, 1962), 7.
27. Borges, "*Deutsches Requiem*," in *Collected Fictions*, 229.
28. Borges, "The Theme of the Traitor and the Hero," in *Fictions*, 143.
29. Daniel Balderston, "'Digamos Irlanda, Digamos 1924': Para repensar la historia en Borges," ["Let's say Ireland, let's say 1924": Rethinking history in Borges], in *Innumerables relaciones: Cómo leer con Borges* [Innumerable relations: How to read with Borges] (Santa Fe: Universidad del Litoral, 2010), 102–18.
30. Paul Ricoeur, *Time and Narrative*, vol. 2, trans. Kathleen McLaughlin and David Pellauer (Chicago: University of Chicago Press, 1986), 247.
31. Borges, "A New Refutation of Time," in *Selected Non-fictions*, 323.

BIBLIOGRAPHY

SELECTED WORKS BY BORGES

While a complete bibliography of Borges's works is beyond this scope of this text, to help readers find the most useful editions for their own research, this list includes the major works discussed in this book. It includes the original works in Spanish as well as the French and English editions that most of the quotes were taken from.

"Ultraísmo," *Nosotros* (Buenos Aires) 39, no. 151 (December 1921): 466–71.

Fervor de Buenos Aires. Buenos Aires: Imprenta Serantes, 1923.

"Almost a Last Judgment," translated by Stephen Kessler. In *Poems of the Night*. London: Penguin Books, 1925.

Inquisiciones [Inquisitions]. Buenos Aires: Proa, 1925. Reprint. Barcelona: Seix Barral, 1994.

Luna de enfrente [Moon across the way]. Buenos Aires: Proa, 1925.

El tamano de mi esperanza [The full extent of my hope]. Buenos Aires: Proa, 1926. Reprint. Barcelona: Seix Barral, 1994.

El idioma de los argentinos [The language of the Argentines]. Buenos Aires: M. Gleizer, 1928. Reprint. Madrid: Alianza, 1998.

Cuaderno San Martín [San Martin notebook]. Buenos Aires: Proa, 1929.

Evaristo Carriego. Buenos Aires: M. Gleizer, 1930.

Historia universal de la infamia [A universal history of iniquity (or infamy)]. Buenos Aires: Tor, 1935. (The 1954 edition has some new pieces added.)

Historia de la eternidad [A history of eternity]. Buenos Aires: Viau y Zona, 1936.

El jardín de senderos que se bifurcan [The garden of forking paths]. Buenos Aires: Sur, 1941.

Poemas, 1922–1943. Buenos Aires: Losada, 1943.

Ficciones [Fictions]. Buenos Aires: Sur, 1944. (The 1956 edition has some new additions.)

El Aleph. Buenos Aires: Losada, 1949. (Some additions and changes were made to the 1952 and 1957 editions.)

Otras inquisiciones, 1937–1952 [Other inquisitions, 1937–1952]. Buenos Aires: Sur, 1952.

Poemas, 1923–1953. Buenos Aires: Emecé, 1954.

Poemas, 1923–1958. Buenos Aires: Emecé, 1958.

El hacedor [The maker]. Buenos Aires: Emecé, 1960.

Antologia personal [Personal anthology]. Buenos Aires: Sur, 1961.

Macedonio Fernández. Buenos Aires: Ediciones Culturales Argentinas, 1961.

Obra poetica, 1923–1964. Buenos Aires: Emecé, 1964.

Other Inquisitions: 1937–1952. Translated by Ruth L. C. Simms. Austin: University of Texas Press, 1964.

Obra poetica, 1923–1967. Buenos Aires: Emecé, 1967.

Nueva antologia personal [New personal anthology]. Buenos Aires: Emecé, 1968.

El otro, el mismo, 1930–1967 [The other, the same, 1930–1967]. Buenos Aires: Emecé, 1969

El informe de Brodie [Brodie's report]. Buenos Aires: Emecé, 1970.

The Aleph and Other Stories: 1933–1969. Edited and translated by Norman Thomas di Giovanni. New York: E.P. Dutton, 1970.

Historia de la noche [History of the night]. Buenos Aires: Emecé, 1977.

Evaristo Carriego: A Book about Old-Time Buenos Aires. Translated by Norman Thomas di Giovanni. New York: Dutton, 1984.

Atlas. Translated by Anthony Kerrigan. New York: E.P. Dutton, 1985.

Textos cautivos: Ensayos y reseñas en El Hogar *(1936–1939)* [Captive texts: Essays and reviews in *El Hogar*]. Barcelona: Tusquets, 1986.

"Another Poem of the Gifts," translated by Alan Dugan. In *Selected Poems 1923–1967.* London: Penguin, 1989.

Œuvres complètes I [Complete works]. Paris: Gallimard, Bibliothèque de la Pléiade, 1993.

Textos recobrados 1919–1929 [Recovered texts 1919–1929]. Buenos Aires: Emecé, 1997.

Collected Fictions, translated by Andrew Hurley. New York: Penguin, 1998. (Includes the stories from *A Universal History of Iniquity* [1935], *The Garden of Forking Paths* [1941], *Artifices* [1944], *The Aleph* [1949], *The Maker* [1960], *In Praise of Darkness* [1969], *Brodie's Report* [1970], *The Book of Sand* [1975], and *Shakespeare's Memory* [1983].)

Selected Non-fictions. Edited by Eliot Weinberger, translated by Esther Allen, Suzanne Jill Levine, and Eliot Weinberger. New York: Penguin, 1999.

Selected Poems. Edited by Alexander Coleman, translated by Maria Kodama, Willis Barnstone, Alexander Coleman, Stephen Kessler, Kenneth Krabbenhoft, Eric McHenry, W. S. Merwin, Alistair Reid, Hoyt Rogers, Charles Tomlinson, and Alan S. Trueblood. London: Penguin, 1999. (Includes poems from *Fervor de Buenos Aires, Moon across the Way, San*

Martín Copybook, The Maker, The Self and the Other, and more.)
"Metaphors of the 1001 Nights" (from *Historia de la noche*). Translated by Jack Ross. *Magazine* no. 1 (2003): 36–38.

Obras completas I–IV [Complete works I–IV]. Buenos Aires: Emecé, 2007.
On Argentina, edited by Alfred Mac Adam and Suzanne Jill Levine. New York: Penguin, 2010.

BIBLIOGRAPHY

Agamben, Giorgio. *Qu'est-ce que le contemporain?* [What is the contemporary?] Paris: Rivages, 2008.
———. *Stanzas: Word and Phantasms in Western Culture*. Translated by Ronald L. Martinez. Minneapolis: University of Minnesota Press, 1993.
Anzieu, Didier. "Le corps et le code dans les contes de Borges" [The body and the code in Borges's short stories]. In *Le Corps de l'œuvre* [The body of the work]. Paris: Gallimard, 1981.
———. Forward to *Le Secret de Borges* [The secret of Borges], by Julio Woscoboinik. Lyon: Césura Lyon, 1989.
Arendt, Hannah. *Walter Benjamin*. Paris: Allia, 2007.
Balderston, Daniel. "'Digamos Irlanda, Digamos 1924': Para repensar la historia en Borges." ["Let's say Ireland, let's say 1924": Rethinking history in Borges] In *Innumerables relaciones: Cómo leer con Borges* [Innumerable relations: How to read with Borges]. Santa Fe, Argentina: Universidad del Litoral, 2010.
———. *Out of Context: Historical Reference and the Representation of Reality in Borges*. Durham, NC: Duke University Press, 1993.

Barth, John. "The Literature of Exhaustion." *Atlantic*, August 1967: 29–34.
Bayard, Pierre. *Le Plagiat par anticipation* [Plagiarism by anticipation] Paris: Minuit, 2009.
Bioy Casares, Adolfo. *Borges*. Buenos Aires: Destino, 2006.
———. "*El jardín de los senderos que se bifurcan*." [The garden of forking paths] In *Jorge Luis Borges*, edited by Jaime Alazraki, 56–60. Madrid: Taurus, 1976.
Bonnefoy, Yves. Preface to *La Melancolie au miroir: Trois lectures de Baudelaire* [Melancholy in the mirror: Three readings of Baudelaire], by Jean Starobinski. Paris: Julliard, 1989.
Bourdieu, Pierre "L'Illusion biographique" [The biographical illusion]. In *Raisons pratiques: Sur la théorie de l'action*, 81–90. Paris: Seuil, 1994.
Calvino, Italo. *Six Memos for the Next Millennium*. Cambridge, MA: Harvard University Press, 1988.
De Man, Paul. "A Modern Master." *New York Review of Books*, March, 9, 1964.
De Milleret, Jean, and Dominique Roux, eds. *Entretiens* [Interviews]. Paris: Cahier de l'Herne, 1981.

East Irby, James. *Encuentro con Borges* [Encounter with Borges]. Mexico City: Universidad de Mexico, 1962.

Flaubert, Gustave. "Lettre à Louise Colet, June 25–26, 1853." In *Correspondance de Flaubert*, vol. 3. Paris: Édition Conard, 1927.

Foucault, Michel. *The Order of Things: An Archaeology of the Human Sciences*. New York: Taylor and Francis, 2005.

———. "What Is an Author?" In *Modernity and its Discontents*, edited by James Marsh, John D. Caputo, and Merold Westphal. New York: Fordham University Press, 1992.

Freud, Sigmund. "Mourning and Melancholia." In *Collected Papers*, vol. 4, translated by Joan Rivière, 152–70. London: Hogarth Press, 1950.

Gefen, Alexandre. "Dieu supposé (sur les *Vies imaginaires*)" [God imagined (on the *Imaginary lives*]. In *Marcel Schwob d'hier et d'aujourd'hui* [Marcel Schwob of today and yesterday], edited by Christian Berg and Yves Vadé, 194–220. Seyssel: Champ Vallon, 2002.

Genette, Gérard. *Narrative Discourse*. Translated by Jane E. Lewin. Ithaca, NY: Cornell University Press, 1980.

———. *Palimpsests: Literature in the Second Degree*. Translated by Channa Newman and Claude Doubinsky. Lincoln: University of Nebraska Press, 1997.

———. "Utopie Littéraire." In *Figures I*, 123–32. Paris: Seuil, 1966.

Lafon, Michel. *Borges, ou, La réécriture* [Borges, or, rewriting]. Paris: Seuil, 1990.

———. "Le foyer des fictions" [The home of fictions]. *Jorge Luis Borges: Les Essais*. Co-textes 38. Montpellier: Institut de Sociocritique de Montpellier, 2001.

———. "Histoires infâmes, biographies synthétiques, fictions: Vies de Jorge Luis Borges" [Iniquitious stories, synthetic biographies, fictions: Lives of Jorge Luis Borges]. In *Fictions biographiques: xixe-xxie siècles* [Biographical fictions: 19th–21st centuries], edited by Anne-Marie Monluçon and Agathe Salha. Toulouse: Presses Universitaires du Mirail, 2007.

———. *Une vie de Pierre Menard* [A life of Pierre Menard]. Paris: Gallimard. 2008.

Lyon, Thomas E. "Jorge Luis Borges: Selected Bibliography of First Editions and English Translations." *Books Abroad* 45, no. 3 (Summer 1971): 467–69.

Madelénat, Daniel. *La biographie*. Paris: PUF, 1984.

Mannoni, Octave. "Je sais bien, mais quand même" [I know well, but all the same]. In *Clefs pour l'imaginaire, ou, L'autre scène* [Keys to the imaginary, or, The other scene]. Paris: Seuil, 1969.

Molloy, Sylvia. *Las letras de Borges* [The letters of Borges]. Buenos Aires: Sudamericana, 1979.

———. *Signs of Borges*. Durham, NC: Duke University Press, 1994.

Parodi, Cristina. "Borges y la subversión del modelo policial" [Borges and the subversion of the model of the detective novel]. In *Borges: Desesperaciones aparentes y consuelos secretos* [Borges:

Feigned desperation and secret consolation], edited by Rafael Olea Franco, 77–97. Mexico: El Colegio de México, 1999.

Pauls, Alan. *Le facteur Borges* [The Borges factor]. Paris: Christian Bourgois, 2006.

Pezzoni, Enrique. *Enrique Pezzoni, lector de Borges* [Enrique Pezzoni, reader of Borges]. Edited by Annick Louis. Buenos Aires: Sudamerica, 1999.

———. "*Fervor de Buenos Aires*: Autobiografía y autorretrato." (Fervor of Buenos Aires: Autobiography and self-portrait] In *El texto y sus voces* [The text and its voices]. Buenos Aires: Sudamericana, 67–97, 1986.

Piglia, Ricardo. *Crítica y ficción* [Criticism and fiction]. Buenos Aires: Siglo XX, 1990.

———. "Ideología y ficción en Borges" [Ideology and Fiction in Borges]. In *Ficciones Argentinas: Antología de lecuras críticas* [Argentine fictions: Anthology of critical readings], edited by Argentine Literature Research Group of the UBA. Buenos Aires: Norma, 2004.

Ricoeur, Paul. "Fiction and Its Imaginative Variations on Time." In *Time and Narrative*, vol. 3, translated by Kathleen McLaughlin and David Pellauer, 127–42. Chicago: University of Chicago Press, 2010.

———. *Time and Narrative*, vol. 1. Translated by Kathleen McLaughlin and David Pellauer. Chicago: University of Chicago Press, 1990.

———. *Time and Narrative*, vol. 2. Translated by Kathleen McLaughlin and David Pellauer. Chicago: University of Chicago Press, 1986.

Rodríguez Monegal, Emir. *Borges: Hacia una interpretación* [Borges: Toward an interpretation]. Madrid: Guadarrama, 1976.

———. *Jorge Luis Borges: A Literary Biography*. New York: Dutton, 1978.

Rosato, Laura, and Alvarez, Germán, eds. *Borges, libros y lecturas* [Borges, books and readings]. Buenos Aires: Ediciones Biblioteca Nacional, 2010.

Sarlo, Beatriz. *Borges, a Writer on the Edge*. London: Verso, 1995. Available at Borges Studies Online, J. L. Borges Center for Studies and Documentation, https://www.borges.pitt.edu/bsol/bsio.php.

———. *Borges, un escritor en las orillas* [Borges, a writer from the *orillas*]. Buenos Aires: Ariel, 1993.

Schlanger, Judith. "Le précurseur" [The precursor]. In *Le Temps des œuvres: Mémoire et préfiguration* [The time of works: Memory and foreshadowing], edited by Jacques Neefs. Saint-Denis: Presses Universitaires de Vincennes, 2001.

Schwob, Marcel. Preface to *Imaginary Lives*. Translated by Chris Clarke. Cambridge, MA: Wakefield Press, 2018.

Stabb, Martin S. "Introduction: Borges and His Critics." In *Jorge Luis Borges: An Annotated Primary and Secondary Bibliography*, by David William Foster. New York: Garland, 1984, xii–xxxvi. Available at Borges Studies Online, J. L. Borges Center for Studies and Documentation, https://www.borges.pitt.edu/sites/default/files/Stabb.pdf.

Starobinski, Jean. "La mélancolie de l'anatomiste" [The melancholy of the anatomist]. *Tel Quel*, no. 10 (1962): 21–29.

Talese, Gayle. "Argentine Here on Lecture Tour Finds Advantages in Blindness." *New York Times*, February 5, 1962.

Updike, John. "The Author as Librarian." *New Yorker*, October 30, 1965.

Vásquez, María Esther. *Borges: Imágenes, memorias, diálogos* [Borges: Images, memories, dialogues]. Caracas: Monte Avila, 1977.

Ventura, René. *La vraie vie de Pierre Menard, ami de Borges* [The real life of Pierre Menard, friend of Borges]. Nîmes: Lucie Éditions, 2009.

Woscoboinik, Julio. *Le Secret de Borges* [The secret of Borges]. Lyon: Césura Lyon, 1989.

www.ingramcontent.com/pod-product-compliance
Lightning Source LLC
Chambersburg PA
CBHW030656230426
43665CB00011B/1112